ACTIVE PARTICIPATION AT MASS

LIBRARY OF CONGRESS
SURPLUS - 1
DUPLICATE

Active Participation at Mass

*What It Is
And How To Attain It*

LIBRARY
LINCOLN MEMORIAL UNIVERSITY
Harrogate, Tennessee

ANTHONY M. BUONO

220788

ALBA·HOUSE house NEW·YORK
SOCIETY OF ST. PAUL, 2187 VICTORY BLVD., STATEN ISLAND, NEW YORK 10314

BX 2230.2
.B86
1994

Library of Congress Cataloging-in-Publication Data

Buono, Anthony M.
    Active participation at Mass: what it is and how to attain it /
Anthony M. Buono.
        p.   cm.
    ISBN 0-8189-0682-0
    1. Mass. 2. Catholic Church — Liturgy. I. Title.
    BX2230.2.B86   1994
    264'.02036 — dc20
                                                  93-41295
                                                    CIP

Produced and designed in the United States of America by the
Fathers and Brothers of the Society of St. Paul,
2187 Victory Boulevard, Staten Island, New York 10314,
as part of their communications apostolate.

ISBN: 0-8189-0682-0

© Copyright 1994 by the Society of St. Paul

Printing Information:

Current Printing - first digit   1   2   3   4   5   6   7   8   9   10

Year of Current Printing - first year shown

1994   1995   1996   1997   1998   1999

Contents

Foreword

$\mathscr{E}$ver since the liturgical renewal put into effect by the Second Vatican Council some thirty years ago, Catholics have been continually exhorted to active participation in the Mass. We have been told that, among other things, such is not only our right but our responsibility.

The Council stressed the point that people must be aided to achieve participation: "With zeal and patience, pastors of souls must promote the liturgical instruction of the faithful as well as their *active participation* in the Liturgy both internally and externally" (*Constitution on the Sacred Liturgy*, no. 19).

The purpose of this book is to set forth a series of ways in which people can arrive at a fuller participation in the Holy Sacrifice of the Mass. The ways detailed are those that seem in my estimation to be most effective. Still, they are only some ways and are not meant to be exclusive or exhaustive.

These suggestions are the result of years of work in liturgical publishing and a stint spent as chairman of a Parish Liturgy Committee. A few of them (through talks and articles) have already helped some people to participate more fully in the Liturgy. But this is the first time they have appeared under the covers of a single book.

It is my hope that put in this form they will aid a wider audience to achieve the active participation that the Church has characterized as the right and the duty of all Catholics by reason of their universal priesthood.

Chapter 1

Recognizing
a Sacramental World

*M*any Catholics go through life never really knowing or making use of the wonderful means for salvation that Christ has placed at our disposal through his Church. We live secularized lives in a secular world, hardly realizing that Jesus has made it a sacramental world — "Behold, I make all things new" (Revelation 21:5) — a world in which every activity and every event can be a means of divine grace leading to salvation.

God communicates himself to us through gestures, words, and things, which we term Sacramentals. They are actions of God through the Spirit. God's primary sacramental gesture was to become man. Hence, Jesus is the first and true Sacrament, because he is the efficacious sign of the divinization of humankind. Through his

1

life, death, and resurrection, Jesus enabled us to encounter the Triune God and share in his own divine life.

Indeed, all the actions of Jesus during his earthly life are ultimately intended to give life — eternal life. This is the message of the resurrection: "I am the Resurrection and the Life; whoever believes in me, even should he die, will live" (John 11:25).

The Church — Sacrament of the Encounter with Christ

For the benefit of those who did not live in his day, Jesus established the Church as the Sacrament of encounter with him. Through the Church, Jesus continues to be active in the world and to communicate with all human beings.

The Church is the Mystical Body of Christ; he is its head, we are its members. As such the Church is a sign, a Sacrament, of Christ. She proclaims Christ, and it is in her that Christ is encountered.

This union with Christ and through him with God constitutes the Kingdom of God. The Church recognizes the Kingdom already present in the world. She embraces it in joy and thanksgiving. She labors to extend it to all peoples and does this through the Sacraments.

The Sacraments rightly celebrated bring

the hope of the Church to the world. They are advance signs of the success and completion of the world in Christ Jesus. Thus, just as the Incarnate Christ was the visage of the Father, so the Church is the visage of the risen and ascended Christ for all people on earth. She is the efficacious sign, the Sacrament, that renders him present to the world.

Thus, the Church enables us to encounter Christ in his Sacraments. These touch the major points of our lives and sanctify them. They all revolve around the Mass, also termed the Eucharist.

The Eucharist — Christifying the Universe

To obtain a true idea of the role of the Eucharist in our lives, we must see the world with the eyes of the Bible. We will then realize that humankind is the chosen instrument of our Redemption. Christ came to endure pain, to suffer and die in the flesh; and he rose in the flesh. Hence, flesh and inanimate matter are associated with the Savior's mission and his victory over death.

We can utilize all the resources of the universe in working out our salvation. In the words of the First Eucharistic Prayer at Mass, "Through [Christ] you give us all these gifts. You fill them with life and goodness. You bless them and make them holy."

We must become imbued with the awareness that, as the Bible shows, human beings master the cosmos and by their daily undertakings perfect the divine image in themselves. Through their work and social interaction, they attain a community of interpersonal relationships based on love. "God is love, and he who abides in love abides in God and God in him" (1 John 4:16). We become one with God through love.

This takes place principally through what we call Liturgy, by which God is worshiped and glorified and we are made sharers in the life and Kingdom of God. (1) In the Mass, the divine-human Jesus through the action of his Spirit enables us to partake of his divine life. (2) We participate in this sacred action with the wondrous power of our reason, sentiments, emotions, and physical senses—hearing, singing, speaking, tasting, and so forth. (3) Inanimate creation also has a role to play: bread, wine, oil, lights, incense, vestments, chalice, bells, organ.

In the final analysis, through the Liturgy, Christ becomes one with the members of his Mystical Body. The sanctification of the world falls under his influence through our free cooperation prompted by grace. In a sense, we ourselves are the substance offered and transformed in the Mass and, through us, the world is offered and transformed in its development each day. The bread (body) symbolizes what creation succeeds in producing. The wine (blood) symbolizes what creation causes to be lost in exhaustion and suffering in the course of its effort.

The transubstantiation of bread and wine into the body, blood, soul and divinity of Christ is extended into the world and embraces the totality of the joys and pains that result from this divinely ordained developing process. Christ gathers up all the joys and sufferings and offers them to the Father. He causes them to become salvific for all who experience them.

As a result, we can say that the Mass includes a true consecration of humankind. The entire world is offered and transformed by Christ's saving grace through the mediation of the Church in the Mass. Or put another way, the saving merits won by Christ through his passion, death and resurrection are applied to the world and everything in it here and now. This consecration takes place in a sacramental manner — which is therefore imperfect and calls for completion. Christ has accomplished the definitive act of offering. But for the Christian community and for the world, the sacrifice will not be fully accomplished until the end of time.

Liturgy — Public Worship of the Church

All this is accomplished through the Liturgy, especially the Mass. "The sacred liturgy... is the public worship that our Redeemer, the

Head of the Church, offers to the heavenly Father, and that the community of Christ's faithful pays to its Founder, and through him to the eternal Father; it is, in short, the whole public worship rendered by the Mystical Body of Jesus Christ, Head and members" (Pius XII, *Encyclical on the Sacred Liturgy*, no. 20).

This is the classic definition of Liturgy, repeated by the *New Code of Canon Law* (Canon 834). Yet for most of us, Liturgy is a rather formidable word, a word we hardly ever use in everyday speech.

Originally, this word denoted a voluntary work done for the people. The Greek translation of the Jewish Scriptures completed in the 3rd century B.C. and known as the Septuagint turned this word into a reference to the priestly worship carried on in the Temple.

The early Church utilized it for a service of worship in which each member of the community offers to God on behalf of all in accord with his or her role. By the Middle Ages, it came to denote the official worship of the Church.

Thus, Liturgy is a divine work entrusted to the people of God. It is the carrying on of the work of Christ by his Church in union with him.

Those who were not privileged to encounter Christ in his earthly life can now encounter him in his glorified state through the Liturgy and can unite with him in his sacrifice to the Father made once and for all.

Viewed in this way, Liturgy is partially divested of its formidable character. It comes across to us as it truly is: a key to life, a call to union, a blessing brimming with gifts, a petition filled with hope, the extension of the Paschal Mystery (which is the passion, death and resurrection of Jesus) to all ages and all peoples, and indeed to the whole universe.

Through our Baptism that made us universal priests, it is our privilege as Christians to be able to take part in this prayer of the Church. It is our privilege to take part in this prayer (a) through a hierarchical order that is essential to it. But it is likewise our privilege to take part in this prayer (b) in a communal fashion as members of the Church community. It is our privilege to be sanctified by this prayer (c) through our insertion into Christ's Paschal Mystery. Finally, it is our privilege to be instructed by this prayer (d) as part of those to whom God speaks through Christ in the Spirit.

Characteristics of the Liturgy

The Mass (like all sacramental rites) may be termed a dialogue between God and his people. Even more, it is a ritual in which God acts and his people become involved. In this communication, the Mass makes use of signs as well as words. It involves bodily attitudes, incorporates gestures, utilizes things, is performed in places, blesses objects and consecrates them.

Some of these are natural signs, making use of the images and symbols already present in creation which have a certain resonance in the human heart. Most of them, however, are biblical signs. They are the signs that Jesus himself used when he instituted the Mass and the Sacraments as well as those that the rest of the Scriptures show as being used by our predecessors in the Catholic Faith.

As a matter of fact, the Mass has been called the Bible in action, for the Bible permeates every part of the rites. The Mass includes Bible passages (readings), Bible chants (antiphons and hymns), Bible formulas (greetings, acclamations, and institution narrative), Bible allusions (prayers), and Bible instruction (homily) as well as extemporaneous prayers of the individual community that are Bible-inspired.

The principal celebrant of the Mass is Christ himself. The secondary celebrant is the bearer of the official priesthood who stands at the altar "in persona Christi." "The priest-celebrant, putting on the person of Christ, alone offers sacrifice, and not the people, nor the clerics, not even the priests who reverently assist. All, however, can and should take an active part in the sacrifice" (*AAS* 48, 711ff; *The Christian Faith*, no. 1572, p. 476).

In the Mass each person has an office to perform as a result of the universal priesthood received at Baptism. The people take their part by means of acclamations, responses, psalmody, antiphons, and songs as well as by actions, gestures, bodily attitudes, and a reverent silence at the proper times.

The Mass contains instruction in the faith, for the Church teaches as she sanctifies. "In the readings, explained by the homily, God is speaking to his people, opening up to them the mystery of redemption and salvation, and nourishing their spirit; Christ is present to the faithful through his own word. Through the chants the people make God's word their own and through the profession of faith affirm their adherence to it. Finally, having been fed by this word, they make their petitions in the general intercessions for the needs of the Church and for the salvation of the whole world" (*General Instruction of the Roman Missal*, no. 33).

Most important of all, however, is the fact that the Mass requires participation. Without participation, we get nothing from the Mass. What this participation may be and how we achieve it will be shown in subsequent chapters.

Chapter 2

Understanding
What Participation Is

*W*hat does it mean to participate (take part) in something? Broadly speaking, it means to become personally involved in it according to the make-up and rules (explicit or implicit) of the event.

If a person attends a baseball game and instead of keeping score pulls out a radio and musical score and spends all his or her time listening to an opera, that person (though physically present at the ball park) has no participation in the game at all.

The same lack of participation characterizes a person who attends a cocktail party and sits in a corner with a novel paying no attention to anyone else.

Participation at Mass means to take part in the celebration/memorial of the saving mystery of Christ. By such participation Christians lay internal and faith-filled hold of the redemptive action of the risen Jesus present through the power of the Holy Spirit.

By this contact, we are made holy and render to God true worship in spirit and in truth (John 4:26). In the words of Pius X, "The active participation of the people in the worship of the Church is the primary and indispensable source of the Christian spirit."

Even though it is true that "every time the priest re-enacts what the divine Redeemer did at the Last Supper the sacrifice is really accomplished... for he who offers it acts in the name both of Christ and of the faithful of whom the divine Redeemer is the Head..., and this happens whether the faithful are present... or whether they are absent" (*Mediator Dei*; see *The Christian Faith*, no. 1569, p. 475), participation at Mass remains one of the constitutive elements of the Eucharistic Celebration. Only with such participation is there realized in full manner the end that the Mass pursues — the glorification of God and the sanctification of human beings.

"We Are the Church"

Active participation at Mass was an intensely personal part of the experience of the Christians of antiquity, insistently encouraged by the Fathers of the Church. Then, for a variety of reasons, it declined from the time of the Middle Ages onward. The people were left pretty much to their own devices. Many times they felt themselves to be perfect strangers at the sacrifice, often even being deprived of the sight of the altar on account of the walls and rood lofts that set off the choir.

This is one of the factors that led many Catholics before Vatican II to think of the Mass as a function solely of the hierarchy: the pope, bishops, and priests. For them, it was something presided over by the clergy while the laity looked on passively, joining their intentions to the action on the altar and receiving the fruits stemming from it.

Over the centuries, the laity lost all sense of being the Church, God's People of the New Covenant. They thought of themselves as merely belonging to the Church. They were simply those upon whom the Church exercised her apostolate. In short, they were the raw material of the Church's work.

Prior to Vatican II, the concept of the Church as the Body of Christ, which was so familiar to the early Christians, came to the fore again. In the words of Pius XII, "The laity do not belong to the Church; they are the Church!"

The Church is, in a certain sense, Christ still living on in this world throughout the ages, ever engaged in saving and sanctifying people of every generation. And her role as such is most clearly revealed when a full complement of God's holy people, united in prayer and in a common liturgical service (especially the Mass), exercises a thorough and active participation.

Each local assembly represents the visible Church constituted throughout the world, that is, the Universal Church. It is the Church in miniature, a manifestation of the whole Church. It is the Church made actual at a definite time and place, acting in the name of the Universal Church whenever it celebrates the Mass.

In the words of Vatican II: "The Liturgy is the summit toward which the activity of the Church is directed; at the same time it is the fountain from which all her power flows" (*Constitution on the Sacred Liturgy*, no. 10). By means of the Mass, grace is channeled to us, and our sanctification in Christ and the glorification of God are prayerfully achieved.

More Than Devout Attendance

For the first time in her history the Church has officially spelled out that the people are central to the celebration of the Mass. They have key roles and those are now indicated in the official liturgical books. The members of the assembly are not mere spectators but active participants:

"The Church... earnestly desires that Christ's faithful, when present at this Mystery of Faith, should not be there as strangers or silent spectators. On the contrary, through a good understanding of the rites and prayers they should take part in the sacred action, conscious of what they are doing, with devotion and full collaboration" (*Constitution on the Sacred Liturgy*, no. 48).

We are called to pray, to sing, to perform certain actions and take certain positions. And it is as a group that we are to respond. This common participation must be more than mere outward conformity for the sake of good order. It must be motivated by a deep religious sense of our relationship to one another and to God in Christ as well as of our office to be a sign of the Mystery of the Church.

When we are present at Mass, we need more than just devout attendance. We must be actively present. Indeed, participation at Mass is both the right and the duty of the faithful. We are thus enabled to exercise whatever share in Christ's priesthood has been conferred on us — either the priesthood of the faithful through the Sacrament of Baptism or the ministerial priesthood through the Sacrament of Holy Orders.

Unfortunately, most of the faithful still seem to be afflicted with a spectator mentality. Regardless of the emphasis on participation in our contemporary world — on getting out and doing things — they are perfectly content to be present at Mass with devout attendance.

This attitude stems from a belief that in the

Church there are two distinct classes of people — those who minister and those who are ministered to. It thinks of worship as something performed in the sanctuary by the ministers while the recipients of ministry are merely present in the pews.

Active participation, on the other hand, flows from the knowledge that in the Church all are ministers (though with diverse roles and offices). This view looks upon worship as carried out by all as the act of all and for all. In other words, it regards the laity not only as being present at the act of worship but also as being the "co-celebrants" of the liturgical celebration. The priest, in fact, asks us to "Pray, brethren, that *our* [joint] sacrifice may be acceptable to God, the almighty Father."

Without this unique insight, the Eucharist seems something apart from us. But if we are there as those who belong, we will make it our own. We will participate in the sacred action with words and gestures, mind and will.

We know that it is Christ who celebrates the Mass through the ministry of the ordained priest. We must also realize that the people associate themselves in the celebration in strict accord with the liturgical function proper to each.

Qualities of Participation

The Council in its *Constitution on the Sacred Liturgy* outlined the basic qualities of participation in the Liturgy, and especially the Mass.

It must be full, conscious, active, and fruitful (nos. 11, 14, and 41), internal and external (nos. 19 and 110), in accord with the age, condition, way of life and degree of culture (no. 19) of the whole assembly (no. 121), acting in a correct and ordered manner (see nos. 28-29).

Thus, our participation must be both internal and external. It must have an inner spirituality that is the soul of our external participation and that must conform uniquely to the truth of the sanctification of the faithful and the glory of the Trinity.

This requires a personal response on our part in the unique mystical presence of the Church to the call of the Father in, with, and through Christ by the power of the Spirit.

Our participation must also be full. We must respond by being perfectly attuned to the objective of the celebration, giving full reign to the possibilities of the supernatural activities that form part of our supernatural existence as people deputed for the worship of God. It must engage our whole person with all the faculties required: mind, heart, and soul as well as body with tongue and lips, hands and feet, and so forth.

Our participation must be conscious. We must take part fully aware of what we are doing, actively engaged in the rite, and enriched by its effects. The prayer of the Church is not divorced from our understanding. It goes out to meet our eagerness to know and comprehend; it fulfills the word of Christ: "They shall all be taught by God" (John 6:45).

Our participation must be active, that is, it must be much more than simple assistance, no matter how attentive that may be. We must not be simple spectators, no matter how interested. We must be doers in the action — responding, praying, worshiping!

In addition, our participation must be communitarian. This is demanded by the intrinsic nature of the Mass as well as for its psychological effectiveness. Liturgical services are not private functions but celebrations of the Church, the holy people of God united with their bishops and priests.

Finally, our participation must be hierarchically structured. Since the Mass is a manifestation of the Church, it must possess a quality that is intrinsic to the nature of the Church, which is hierarchical. Just as the Church is composed of members who differ in function, so too is the liturgical assembly.

The Church as an organized body, a living society, prays as an assembly in which each member has a role to fulfill. All are to take part in the drama, but not in the same roles. Priest, deacon, reader, chanter, faithful — all perform in turn and listen in turn.

The Result of Personal Openness

The minimum required for participation is physical presence, corporal attitude, unity of gesture and movement, unison of words, and common action without mentioning other more profound dimensions that affect the laws of grace and the communication of divine life.

Then there is personal openness to the community itself and to the Mystery being celebrated. If we do not open ourselves from the beginning — this is the function of the Introductory Rites — we will only with difficulty welcome the Word of God and enter into communication with the Mystery.

Personal openness requires a climate of communication and interchange, so that a sharing of attitudes and sentiments will be achieved on the horizontal level, which will in turn lead to a vertical communication with the Father in Jesus and in the Holy Spirit.

This common action requires the renunciation of personal manners of expression so as to make use only of the admonitions that the Liturgy offers as regards attitudes, words, and gestures as well as formulas of prayer and chants. This is not a question of annulling the individual and the personal but of integrating it in an horizon of common participation.

We must overcome the confrontation between person and community so that we may have access to that "common sacred" which in the Church is always the Mystery of Christ, the gift of salvation present and operative in the liturgical celebrations.

The actions and prayers that form the celebration of the sacrament pertain to an economy of salvation that has been revealed by God and includes precise gestures and words. These have in themselves a reality and salvific efficacy that transcend the prayers of any one individual.

The word reminds us of the Word of God that is announced and proclaimed and gives meaning to the signs and actions of the rite. It also recalls the word of the assembly and the ministers who pray, sing, and act in response to God and to actualize what they are celebrating (see Vatican II, *Constitution on Divine Revelation*, nos. 33, 30).

Hence, we can say that in the celebration each action is really a word, each rite a phrase, and the combination a message of salvation interchanged, communicated, and shared.

The liturgical action is based on the material and spiritual nature of human beings. Often reduced nowadays to an object or a number, disintegrated and decomposed by the protocols of a modern civilization that esteems or seeks only one part of us, we are in reality a composite whole. One in body and soul, we represent the material universe, as we raise our voices in praise of the Creator.

Central to the sacrificial ritual of the Mass

is the humanity of Christ. On coming into the world, our Redeemer said: "Sacrifice and sin offering you did not desire, but a body you prepared for me" (Hebrews 10:5). Christ assumes our humanity and converts it into a sacrament of our salvation (see *Constitution on the Sacred Liturgy*, no. 5).

Therefore, in liturgical celebrations every action has the function of a sacrament and is transformed into an event that evokes and actualizes in its own way the Paschal Mystery of Christ, affecting us in the totality of our being and embracing our entire existence.

Genuine Involvement and Response

On the other hand, the action has the task of expressing our response as human beings to the action of God in our lives. This response, which consists essentially in conversion and faith, stirred up by the Word of God and nourished and sustained by the rites, constitutes our essential collaboration in the full efficacy of the liturgical and sacramental action:

"The uniformity in standing, kneeling, or sitting to be observed by all taking part is a sign of the community and the unity of the assembly; it both expresses and fosters the spiritual attitude of those taking part" (*General Instruction of the Roman Missal*, no. 20).

Participation requires that actions must be

performed with dignity, clarity, truth, and authenticity. In spite of the precariousness and poverty of our human condition, always subject to the temptation of routine and automatism or lack of expressivity, our gestures are a sensible and essential element of our sanctification and the worship of God, which are the two goals of the Liturgy.

We cannot forget that liturgical participation requires in both faithful and ministers the exercise of cultic attitudes that are specifically Christian rather than merely religious. The peculiarity of the Christian Liturgy, which embraces all existence and transforms it into worship of the Father in Spirit and in truth, requires that there be no rupture between celebration and life, between worship and moral conduct.

Failure to keep this correlation is at the bottom of many inhibiting, individualistic, and pietistic attitudes that impede participation. In order to participate, we must cultivate generosity and solidarity, which will be translated into communion in the heart of the Liturgy. The consequences will be manifested later in the testimony of our lives, in personal spiritual growth, in the mission and apostolate of the Church.

Chapter 3

Carrying Out
the People's Parts

*O*ne of the surest and simplest ways to participate at Mass is to pay close attention to the
"People's Parts" and carry them out diligently. In
other words, we can participate best by taking our
rightful part in the celebration.

"All in the assembly gathered for Mass,
have an individual right and duty to contribute
their participation in ways differing according to
the diversity of their order and liturgical function. Thus in carrying out this function, all,
whether ministers or laypersons, should do all
and only those parts that belong to them, so that
the very arrangement of the celebration itself
makes the Church stand out as being formed in a
structure of different orders and ministries" (*General Instruction of the Roman Missal*, no. 58).

The Mass is composed of an Ordinary and

a Proper. The Ordinary is the part of the Mass that remains unchanged from day to day.

The Proper contains the texts that vary according to the liturgical seasons (Advent, Christmas, Lent, Easter, and Ordinary Time) or according to the particular feast (of a Saint who was a Martyr, or a Virgin, or a Doctor, and the like).

In both the Ordinary and the Proper there are texts and actions assigned to the different participants in the Mass, that is, to the priest, to the ministers, and to the people.

The Mass is divided into two major divisions: the Liturgy of the Word and the Liturgy of the Eucharist.

In the Liturgy of the Word, we exercise our role by encountering Christ in the proclamation of God's Word and by preparing for and responding to that Word. In the Liturgy of the Eucharist, we exercise our role by actively participating in the renewal of the sacrifice of the Cross through our acclamations and responses as well as by our intimate union with the glorified Lord in Communion.

The Mass is further divided into five minor divisions (also called parts): the first two in the Liturgy of the Word and the last three in the Liturgy of the Eucharist. They are: (1) Introductory Rites; (2) Proclamation of the Word; (3) Preparation of the Gifts; (4) Eucharistic Prayer; and (5) Communion Rite.

The People's Parts occur in every one of these five divisions of the Mass. Furthermore, these parts are so structured as to elicit definite sentiments from the people and ensure the full participation of the assembly.

Introductory Rites — Keynote

The Entrance Song (or Entrance Antiphon, which replaces it when there is no singing) customarily sets the tone for the day's celebration. We acclaim Jesus (in the person of the priest) who comes to reenact and re-present his saving sacrifice for us and to invite us to participate in his sacrificial meal — to become one in him.

Then we exchange greetings with the priest and ask God to purify us so that we may worthily hear his Word and celebrate his Eucharist. In addition, by means of this Penitential Rite we ask forgiveness of one another so that we may offer this Mass with complete solidarity.

We then proceed to utter several beautiful and ancient texts that express praise, adoration, and thanksgiving: the Kyrie, a litany-like plea to Christ for mercy (which because of its structure is used in the Penitential Rite) and the Gloria whose corpus is a lyrical praise of the Incarnate Son, our Redeemer and Intercessor with the Father. Addressed to the Father, it concludes giving praise to the Trinity.

The priest concludes the Introductory Rites

220788

by reciting the Opening Prayer in our name. Through our response ("Amen"), we assent to all that has gone before. By this prayer we gather together the sentiments expressed in the Entrance Antiphon (or Song) and, in the name of Jesus Christ, refashion them into a formal petition to the Father.

Proclamation of the Word — Response

The proclamation of the Word now takes place, bringing Christ into our midst. During this part of Mass, we have an Ordinary response after each of the three readings ("Thanks be to God" after the first two and "Praise to you, Lord Jesus Christ" after the third), two Ordinary dialogue responses at the beginning of the Gospel ("And also with you"; "Glory to you, Lord Jesus Christ"), and two Proper chants. The latter, sometimes termed Intervenient Chants, are the Responsorial Psalm and the Alleluia (or Gospel Acclamation).

The Responsorial Psalm is our official response to the First Reading (usually taken from the Prophets of the Old Testament or from the Letters of the Apostles of the New Testament). It is our praise for the wondrous works God has done on our behalf.

The Alleluia looks forward to the Gospel message. It is an acclamation for the Christ who becomes present among us during the proclamation of God's Word. It constitutes our climactic utterance during the Liturgy of the Word.

Indeed, scholars who study the Liturgy regard these Intervenient Chants as the most important Proper Parts of the People. For they are directly responsive and introductory to God's Word, which is the highlight of the first major division of the Mass.

We now go to encounter Christ as he becomes present in the proclamation of his Gospel. This point is underscored by the response after the Gospel: "Praise to you, Lord Jesus Christ." It is to Christ that we are speaking. It is Christ that we have encountered.

After listening reverently to God's Word, we listen to the updating of that Word to our circumstances of life by the Homily that is preached. We then indicate our acceptance of this Word in the recitation of the Nicene Creed — an Ordinary part that dates back to the 4th century.

Here too prayers are interspersed relating this part of the Mass to actual circumstances: these make up the Prayer of the Faithful. When correctly composed, the list of petitions takes its starting point from the Bible texts just proclaimed and the response just elicited. In that way we can readily assent to the sentiments expressed by the Amen uttered at the end of the concluding prayer said by the priest. By this same Amen, we also assent to all that has taken place during this division of the Mass.

Preparation of the Gifts — Offering

We open the second major division of Mass (Liturgy of the Eucharist) with an Ordinary processional chant that introduces and sets the tone for the Preparation of the Gifts. At the same time a few members of the assembly bring the gifts of bread and wine as well as the sacred vessels to the altar where the sacrifice of the Mass will be offered. The bread and wine are our gifts to God that will be turned into his Gift (Jesus) to us.

They also represent all the monetary gifts that we offer for the good of the community (for Liturgy, counseling, education, and the like). Even more important, they incorporate all the joys and sorrows that the present day or coming week will bring for us and the community as a whole.

Just before the end of this division, we are exhorted by the priest to join wholeheartedly in the sacrifice, which is ours as well as his: "Pray, brethren, that our sacrifice may be acceptable to God, the almighty Father." And we immediately utter our affirmative response: "May the Lord accept this sacrifice at your hands for the praise and glory of his name, for our good, and the good of all his Church." We put into words what we have already symbolized by our gifts in the Offertory Procession.

Finally, the priest adds the "summing-up" Prayer Over the Gifts in the name of the whole assembly. It is usually related to the Offertory

Song. As we voice our Amen, we assent to the Prayer and to all that has preceded in this division of the Mass.

Eucharistic Prayer — Encounter

The Introductory Dialogue (part of the Ordinary) helps us get into the spirit of the "Heart of the Mass," the Eucharistic Prayer. The priest invites us to praise and thank God; we give our prompt response that it is both right and good to do so.

In addition to the overriding reasons found in Salvation History, the Preface lists other special reasons for praising God on a given day. We join our sentiments to those given in the Preface by voicing another praise of God with the magnificent Ordinary part known as the Holy, Holy, Holy. We stress that the earth as well as heaven is filled with God's glory — and that glory will increase as we continue with this Eucharist.

We go on to join the priest silently as he calls upon the Holy Spirit to bless our sacrifice and make it holy as we enter the narrative of the Last Supper. By it we are given, as it were, a front seat at the Lord's Institution of the Mass. The priest in Christ's person repeats the words and actions of the Lord, enabling us to encounter Jesus at the high point of his sacrificial giving on earth.

Christ becomes present in a new and wonderful way, and we address him in the beautiful words of another Ordinary part, the Memorial Acclamation. We should do all we can to pronounce them with outward reverence and inner conviction.

The four formularies that may be used sum up what the Mass is all about. Christ has redeemed us in history. He is with us now in mystery. He will come to us again in glory. Every Mass is our little Easter.

The Eucharistic Prayer recalls the saving events of Christ and then lists the "us" for whom the sacrifice is being offered; the servants of God, our relatives, friends, and benefactors who are Christians as well as all people, living and dead.

The Concluding Doxology gives glory to the Father, through the Son, in the Holy Spirit. We voice our complete endorsement of this sentiment through our "Great Amen" (Ordinary part). We assent to all that has gone before. We have encountered Christ. We now want to offer ourselves to the Father with, through, and in him, and we eagerly look forward to our union with him in Communion.

Communion Rite — Union

We prepare for Communion by reciting the Our Father, the responses to the Prayer for Peace, the Sign of Peace, and the Lamb of God (a prayer for pardon and peace), while the priest makes a quiet preparation for Communion. Then with him we acknowledge our unworthiness to receive such a Visitor in the words of the centurion of the Gospel: "Lord, I am not worthy...."

It is at this point that the Communion Antiphon (or Communion Song), which governs this division, is recited or sung. This text provides us with the particular nuance for the reception of Communion each day. It allows us to vary our reflections for receiving Christ from day to day in accord with the Liturgical Year.

After Communion the priest performs the ablutions, and a Period of Silence follows — for personal or public thanksgiving. Then the priest says the Prayer after Communion in the name of all. It sums up the sentiments of those present inspired by the Communion Antiphon. We concur in these sentiments by our Amen, which also gives our assent to all that has been done in this division of Mass.

The priest then blesses the assembly and sends us forth to bring Christ into our daily lives and relationships. We respond with a final word of assent, "Thanks be to God," and sing a Recessional Song, officially closing the celebration in a customary way.

A careful look at the points made above will demonstrate the many helps that are built into the Mass itself to enable us to participate in it. All we need do is pay attention and be of goodwill. The rite of the Church will do the rest.

Chapter 4

Utilizing Ways
to Better Participation

*A*s in many other areas of human existence, there is no set way of achieving better participation at Mass. Each of us is free to make use of whatever works for us. Nonetheless, there are ways that seem to help many of us. The following tips indicate some of them.

1. *Be Aware of the Power of the Mass.* We must be convinced that the Mass matters! It is the summit and fount of our Christian existence. It enables us to worship God fittingly, to encounter Christ personally, and to gain strength for living our faith.

Similarly, we must be convinced that our participation in each Mass also matters. Each of us has been given something to contribute to every Eucharist we take part in, something no one else in the community can offer. By our unique participation in each Eucharist we bring

Christ's peace and love into our life situation.

2. *Prepare before Mass*. We must realize that no one — priest, minister, or member of the congregation — can take part in the Mass properly without adequate preparation. Therefore, we must strive to prepare ourselves during the previous week and immediately before Mass.

We must first of all admit that we are in constant need of God's mercy and grace. Then we should become familiar with the Scripture readings as well as the prayers of the upcoming Mass. We should dress appropriately in our Sunday best because we are coming into the presence of him who is King of kings and Lord of lords. St. Paul exhorts us to glorify God in our bodies (1 Corinthians 6:20), and among other ways, we do this by being properly attired for our Sunday worship.

We are going to use our physical senses to hear God's Word, to observe the ritual acts, to smell the fragrance of incense, flowers, and candles, to walk in procession, to reach out for and eat the Bread of life and drink the Cup of salvation, to touch the hand of a brother or sister at the Sign of Peace, and to enjoy the sound of sacred music.

3. *Make Use of Participation Aids*. In every church there are usually participation aids — a Missalette and/or a song book — that give the People's Parts. We should make use of them.

Better still, we should obtain a Sunday

Missal, which contains all the texts of the Sunday Masses and familiarize ourselves with them beforehand. The better we know what is coming at each celebration, the deeper will be our participation. The more familiar we are with the specific mystery of Christ being recalled in a particular Mass, the more likely we are to become wholly immersed in it.

4. *Keep in Touch with the Assembly*. The Mass is never our own private preserve. It is always the worship of the whole Church, carried out by local churches in community. Everything we do is done in union with the other members of the Church.

We should, therefore, do what the assembly does. If there is singing, we should join in with zest. If there is only recitation, we should recite in a clear, measured, and meaningful tone. We should make our voice part of the whole on this particular day.

5. *Join in the Singing*. St. Augustine said: "The person who sings prays twice." Music can assist us and nourish our inner commitment of faith. It enables us to take part in the joy of the redeemed regardless of our life situation.

By joining in the singing we get a sense of unity with all others in the assembly. We function more closely as a group. Because we sing as one voice, we even begin to think and act as one. Listening attentively to the choir is another way of letting singing do its part. It enables us to touch

God, as it were, and often through it we are touched by him.

6. *Utilize the Means of Penance Provided.* We may not receive Communion with a consciousness of grave sin, unrepented and unconfessed. But we should also make use of every means to remove venial sins so that we may approach Holy Communion in the most worthy way possible.

At Mass the Sacramentals that can help in this regard are the prayers of the Penitential Rite, the Lord's Prayer, and the prayers at the reception of Communion. If we use them properly, we will get closer to the purity of soul that the Church desires for all of us.

7. *Take Note of the Visual Aids.* In a real sense, the Mass can be a visual feast. Our churches are built and decorated in a way that makes the assembly conscious of what it is doing.

The sacred vestments and utensils add to the decorum of our worship. They take us out of ourselves, as it were, and conjure up the time of Christ. They can be an effective reminder that we are offering his sacrifice on behalf of all.

Banners provide the theme for the Feast or Season. Richly decorated bindings adorn the sacred books, like the Lectionary from which the Word of God is proclaimed and through which we encounter Christ among us. Flowers around the altar contribute to an air of holy festivity. By letting visuals such as these create their effect on us, we will achieve the proper mood for community worship.

8. *Follow the Processions*. The Mass incorporates five processions —all at key moments and all calculated to manifest the solidarity of the assembly and enhance the participation of its members.

Processions have their foundations in the religious instincts of human beings. They express in marvelous fashion the ordered, calm, trusting, and joyous life, the need for collective prayer and the joy in the victory of our Savior. They translate our walk with Christ on the pilgrimage of life. (See Chapter 8.)

9. *Enter into the Amens*. As we indicated in Chapter 3, the Mass is made up of five minor divisions, each concluded by an Amen — the people's assent to what has gone before. If we become truly aware of this point and make use of it, we can participate more fully in each Mass.

We can join in the priest's prayers in the name of the Church and elicit in ourselves the sentiments that the Memorial of the Lord itself inspires and the Church wishes to instill in us. (See Chapter 5.)

10. *Enlist Both Mind and Body in Your Activity*. Body language is very expressive of our inner sentiments. At Mass we have the occasion to make use of it to enhance our worship. We must realize that body language has great influence on our mental state and vice versa. Body

language is a sign of our inner stance before the Lord.

When we are called to kneel and genuflect, we should be conscious that each is a sign of worship and interior supplication.

When we are encouraged to bow, we should view this act as an act of obeisance before God.

When we are asked to stand at the Gospel and at Communion, our reflection should be that we are showing respect and giving honor to God.

When we fold our hands, we should be aware that this indicates our readiness for prayer.

11. *Speak to the Father in the Prayers.* During the prayers that the priest addresses to God the Father in our name (Opening Prayer, Prayer Over the Gifts, Prayer after Communion, Eucharistic Prayer, and the Oration of the Prayer of the Faithful), we should be aware that we are speaking to our heavenly Father. We should add our own intentions to those formulated in these prayers and be totally submissive to God's will for us indicated in them.

12. *Encounter Jesus in the Readings.* We should be convinced that it is Jesus who comes to speak to us in the Readings as surely as he spoke to the people along the roads of Palestine. He is present to us in his Word being proclaimed as well as in his Sacrament being distributed. He comes to us as our Teacher who leads us to the truth because he is the Way, the Truth and the Life.

Our concern should be to respond positively to the Word we hear proclaimed and explained to us in the Liturgy of the Word and in the Homily. This attitude will inevitably make us better Christians.

13. *Be Inspired by the Spirit.* The Mass (like every Sacrament) takes place in the Spirit. We give glory to the Father through the Son in the Holy Spirit and gain sanctification for ourselves. It is the Spirit who realizes the fruits of the Mass in us and it is the Spirit who is intimately bound up with the transformation of the bread and wine into the Body and Blood of Christ.

Our concern should be to remain completely open to his inspirations so that the Spirit will make of us other Christs.

14. *Grasp the Meaning of Signs.* The Mass is a dialogue, an exchange between God and his people. It makes use of signs that are more eloquent even than speech. It involves bodily postures, specific gestures and actions, the use of material places and things.

In the face of such a preponderance of signs, our task is clear. We must always strive to see behind them and obtain a better, deeper, and clearer understanding of their meaning. We must go beyond them to encounter and contemplate the invisible God whom they represent.

15. *Unite with Jesus in the Eucharistic Celebration.* The Mass is intended to unite us with Jesus and with one another. The most effec-

tive way to do so is for us to accept gratefully what God offers us throughout the Mass: during the Readings and Homily, by being open to God's Word; at the Sign of Peace, by being open to our brothers and sisters in the assembly; and at Communion, by being open to be nourished with the Bread of life and the Cup of unending salvation.

We can then accept Christ back from the Father as our Redeemer and our Head.

16. *Make the Periods of Silence Bear Fruit.* The Mass now includes liturgical periods of silence, each with a particular character. Hence, we should make a great effort to use them wisely.

At the Penitential Rite and after the invitation to pray, we should become recollected. At the conclusion of the Readings or the Homily, we should meditate on God's Word to us. After Communion, we should praise God in our hearts and pray.

At the Prayer of the Faithful, we should make our petitions either by a common response after each petition or by a silent prayer.

At the Eucharistic Prayer, we should observe a religious silence and unite ourselves with the priest who is pronouncing that prayer as the interpreter of the voice of God and the voice of the people who raise their hearts to God.

17. *Pray as a Member of the Communion of Saints.* We must be convinced that we never pray alone. In addition to praying with the mem-

bers of the Church on earth, we also pray with all the Saints who have preceded us. First among these is Mary, the Mother of God, whom we remember at all Eucharists.

We also pray in union with all the Saints who have gone before us in the faith. This is brought home to us especially in the Eucharistic Prayer (in the Preface and the Remembrance of the Saints).

18. *Receive Jesus in Holy Communion.* Communion represents the most important of Christ's four presences at Mass. The others are: his presence in his ministers, his presence in the assembly, and his presence in his Word.

Its main purpose is to make this substantial and personal presence (under the form of Bread and Wine that we eat and drink) the means of our union with him in his sacrifice and also our union with our brothers and sisters who share that presence with us.

19. *Express Thanksgiving after Communion.* Thanksgiving after Communion during Mass is intended to be principally communal in accord with the whole thrust of the Liturgy of the Mass and the reasons for its celebration.

We should carry out that thanksgiving in union with the whole community — by singing the Communion Songs or by reciting the Communion Antiphon or by entering into the spirit of the Period of Silence or Song of Praise after the reception of Communion. Our thanksgiving is communal but in a silent and personal way!

20. *Live the Mass.* We must make sure to advance the legitimate progress of the world during the rest of our day or week. By doing so, we commune with the Mass at its source and carry forward its power to transform all things in Christ.

Thus, our union with Christ at Mass must be expressed in the truth of our lives today — in our actions, in our behavior, in our lifestyle, and in our relationships with others!

In turn the lived Mass will prepare us for our next active participation in the Eucharist.

Chapter 5

Entering Into
the Five Amens

*O*ne of the twenty ways of participating at Mass spoken about in the previous chapter is worth discussing in more detail. For it enables us to participate in a very simple way in each minor division of the Mass.

It involves entering into the spirit of the five Amens. If we make use of none of the other ways, it is possible to participate actively by this way alone, so to speak.

Upon first hearing, this assertion seems too ridiculous to be true. Yet if we put our mind to it and utilize this method, we will discover that it will be of immense help to our participation.

After all, full participation is a tall order. We are so apt to be afflicted with distractions, our attention wanders, the acoustics may be bad, and so forth. We need all the help we can get in achieving the ideal of full, conscious, and active participation.

A Biblical Word

The word "Amen" pervades every part of our liturgical rites, and particularly the Mass. At the same time, it is part and parcel of our everyday lives — for example, when we make the Sign of the Cross. What does it really mean?

"Amen" is a Hebrew word found frequently in the Bible. In the Old Testament it was used to give assent to an oath or to indicate agreement with a good wish or prayer. In the worship carried out in the synagogue, the people used "Amen" to show that they endorsed the prayers recited by the prayer-leader. It signified "truly," "certainly," "so be it."

In the New Testament, Christ made use of this powerful term and gave it a new meaning. He employed it to introduce his statements ("Amen, amen, I say to you...") thereby indicating the absolute truth of what he stated and endorsing that truth with all the weight of his authority.

Accordingly, the word became highly prized by the early Christians. It figured in their private prayers (Romans 1:25; 9:5; 1 Timothy 1:17) and even in the Liturgy — at the end of the celebrant's Eucharistic Prayer (1 Corinthians 14:11). And it has come down to us in that same perspective.

Indeed, "Amen" is used in various ways today. Some congregations of our Separated Brethren use it to punctuate the sermons preached to them. They also employ it to give wholehearted assent to what is said, to profess their adherence to Christ, and to express their joy at being Christians.

When we utter an "Amen" with full awareness, it reveals who we are and what we are doing. It strengthens our prayer, reflects our devotion, reinforces our beliefs, and registers our concern.

The amazing power of this little word was beautifully communicated by Sidney Poitier in his Academy-Award winning role as the handyman Homer Smith in the motion picture *Lilies of the Field*. Poitier's musical and magical rendition of the "Amen" in one of the climactic moments of this magnificent movie was both electric and inspiring. It was a great reminder that our "Amen," too, can do wonders.

Making Each Part of Mass Our Own

As we have seen, the Mass is divided into five minor parts: (1) Introductory Rites; (2) Proclamation of the Word; (3) Preparation of the Gifts; (4) Eucharistic Prayer; and (5) Communion Rite. And at the end of each part there is an "Amen" for us to say.

By concentrating on these Five "Amens," we can make each part of the Mass our own. We can join in the prayers of the priest in the name of the Church and elicit in ourselves the sentiments that the Memorial of the Lord itself inspires and the Church wishes to instill in us.

In short, we can participate fully, actively,

and consciously at every Eucharistic Celebration.

The First "Amen" comes at the end of the Introductory Rites after the priest has said the Opening Prayer, which sums up the liturgical theme of the day and which the first part of Mass is intended to effect in us.

Our "Amen" should mean: We have entered wholly into the preparations for this Eucharist. We are now ready to encounter Jesus as he comes in Word and Sacrament.

The Second "Amen" comes at the end of the Proclamation of the Word after the concluding oration of the Prayer of the Faithful, which is the most direct involvement of our particular community in the Mass.

Our "Amen" should mean: We have received and pondered God's Word and have had it made relevant to us by the Homily and the Prayer of the Faithful. We are now ready to put it into practice in this liturgical celebration and in our lives.

The Third "Amen" comes at the end of the Preparation of the Gifts after the Prayer Over the Gifts, which asks God to receive our offering that is about to be made.

Our "Amen" should mean: We have joined in the preparation of the bread and wine. We are now ready to offer ourselves with Jesus in the sacrifice that is about to be renewed in an unbloody fashion.

The Fourth "Amen" (also known as the Great Amen for it is the most important one we utter at Mass) comes at the end of the doxology that concludes the Eucharistic Prayer with a paean of praise to the Father through, with, and in Christ Jesus, our Lord.

Our "Amen" should mean: We have joined in praising the Father for all his wonderful works and have offered ourselves with Jesus to him. We are now ready to receive Jesus back from the Father in Communion.

The Fifth "Amen" comes at the end of the Prayer after Communion, which thanks God for letting us share in this Eucharist and looks forward to our sharing in the heavenly banquet of the Lamb.

Our "Amen" should mean: We have united ourselves with Jesus and with one another in the sacrificial rite. We are now ready to share the rite with others whom we encounter daily in the hope that we will help them gain an eternal reward.

The Mass moves quickly to a conclusion. Just as the priest at the beginning of the first part greeted the assembly with the invocation of the three Divine Persons, he now blesses the congregation in their Name.

The priest then declares that the assembly is dismissed. There is even an "Amen" at the end of the Blessing, but it is not on the same plane as the previous five.

We should strive to keep the meaning of

each of the Five "Amens" in mind and recall it whenever we are at Mass. Then by pronouncing each "Amen" with full awareness, we will surely make the Mass a more personal part of our daily lives.

Responding with a True "Amen"

Most important of all, we must do all we can to pronounce an "Amen" that is true. We can do so only if we have paid full attention and participated completely in the particular part being concluded. Only then can we really assent to all that has gone before.

We must be convinced that the "Amen" is a most important element. It says that both people and priest have offered this part of the Eucharist and agree on its sentiments. The following points may be of help in this respect.

The ancient rabbis taught that those who pronounced the "Amen" after a blessing were superior to the person who pronounced the blessing. They likened those who said "Amen" to the heroes in battle who always came second, after the shield-bearers who went first.

In addition, the writers of the Talmud listed three erroneous ways of pronouncing the "Amen": furtive, plucked, and orphaned.

A Furtive "Amen" is one stripped of the first vowel (from "Amen" it becomes "uhmen"). A Plucked "Amen" is one like an unripe fruit that is forcefully plucked making it lose the last consonant (from "Amen" it becomes "Ame"). Finally, an Orphaned "Amen" is one pronounced accurately but lacking any relation to the prayer that led to it.

Hence, the writers admonished the people: "Respond neither with a furtive 'amen,' nor with a plucked 'amen,' nor with an orphaned 'amen' or you will reject the blessing with your own mouth.

"Whoever respond with an orphaned 'amen,' may their children be orphans! a furtive 'amen,' may their days be fleeting! a plucked 'amen,' may their days be plucked! But whoever prolong the 'amen,' may their days and years always be prolonged!"

Becoming Christ's "Amen"

A key point for us to remember is that our "Amen" is not an ordinary word. It is not something that we say on our own.

Our "Amen" takes place within the public prayer of the Church and is called for by God's grace. Indeed, it is always uttered in Christ, who is the fulfillment of all God's promises:

"For all God's promises find their 'Yes' in him, which is why it is through Jesus that we say 'Amen' to the glory of God" (2 Corinthians 1:20).

As the true and faithful witness of God's

fidelity to his promises, Christ is God's "Amen," God's "Yes." He is the living "Amen" showing that God is ever willing and able to help us on our journey through life to eternity.

Since this is the case, we should be Christ's "Amen," too. We should make it our responsibility to say a continual "Yes" to Christ and all that he stands for.

In other words, we are to live in such a manner that all our "Amens" will show forth our commitment to Christ and our union with him. We are to be living "Amens."

If we do become living "Amens," our joyous and dedicated "Amens" pronounced in the liturgical assemblies will not be relegated there. They will not be vain sounds but overflow into our everyday lives.

Such living "Amens" will ensure that we are worshiping "in Spirit and in truth" (John 4:23). They will enable us to "put on" Christ and radiate him to others.

Chapter 6

Encountering Christ in the Word of God

*E*very liturgical tradition, whether ancient or modern, has had one theme in common with all others: love, veneration, and use of the Word of God. An ancient Psalm-prayer of the Hispanic-Visigothic Liturgy prays: "Keep our steps from every evil path, O Lord, and let us serve your Word with full attention."

Indeed, the contributions of the Liturgical Movement and the Biblical Renewal led the Second Vatican Council to state that in the celebratory announcement of Holy Scripture Christ is present because in the Word proclaimed during the liturgical action it is Christ who speaks (*Constitution on the Sacred Liturgy*, nos. 1, 7).

The Liturgy of the Word is so intimately connected with the Liturgy of the Eucharist that it constitutes one single act of worship (*Ibid.*, no.

56). This underscores the parallelism between the table of the Word of God and the table of the Body of Christ (*Constitution on Divine Revelation*, no. 21). From both of these tables — though in a different way from each — the faithful derive nourishment for their spiritual life.

The Church is nourished spiritually at the table of God's Word and at the table of the Eucharist: from the former it grows in wisdom and from the latter in holiness. In the Word of God the divine Covenant is announced; in the Eucharist the new and eternal Covenant is renewed. The spoken Word of God brings to mind the History of Salvation; the Eucharist embodies it in the sacramental signs of the Liturgy (*Prologue to Order of Readings for Mass*, Second Typical Edition, no. 10).

To deal with the "celebration" of the Word of God is equivalent to dealing with one of the most significant presences of Christ in our midst after his Eucharistic presence and his presence in our brothers and sisters. It is one of the major sources of nourishment for our faith. There is an illuminating and specific vitality emanating from the Word of God which the Church through its "prayed faith" is daily rediscovering and appreciating ever more.

Liturgical Meaning of God's Word

The privileged place for proclaiming the Word of God is within the worshiping community as it confesses and celebrates the Mystery of Salvation. Indeed it was in the confessing and celebrating community that the Word of God had its origin and took its life, first through the Old Testament in synagogal reading, study, and prayer; then through the New Testament, in the proclamations and the Liturgy of the Church.

In the course of the Liturgy, the Word of God comes alive. It ceases to be a simple story of the past and becomes my story. The promises of God made to his people are promises made also to me; the prayer of the people of God becomes my prayer; the wondrous works of God in favor of his people are renewed on my behalf.

The Mass is the perfect forum for God's Word to be proclaimed, understood, and loved. It presents the ideal background for the interpretation of God's Word. In each celebration of the Liturgy, the Word of God is converted into a "new happening," a "new event." And it takes on "new meaning and power" in keeping with the seasons of the liturgical year, the feasts, or the particular celebration (see *Ibid.*, no. 3).

The liturgical celebration of God's Word is more than a gathering for study or catechetical formation making use of a text from Sacred Scripture. It is a salvific event in which God speaks to his people today — to this concrete community!

Through its "today" and "here," the celebration itself gives new meaning and power to the word contained in the sacred books. This is what Jesus himself indicated in his homily at Nazareth (Luke 4:16-21): "Today this Scripture has been fulfilled in your hearing" (see also Luke 24:25-35 and 44-49).

"Thus the same text may be read or used for diverse reasons on diverse occasions and celebrations of the liturgical year" (*Ibid.*, no. 3, note 7).

Christ's Presence in His Word

The revealed Word is always living and effective. It does not cease to record and prolong salvation. And it achieves its greatest expression and saving power within the liturgical celebration. The reason for this is not hard to discover.

Christ is present and active when the Word is proclaimed in the community. Carrying out the Mystery of Salvation, he sanctifies us and offers perfect worship to his Father.

What was of greatest importance in Christ has been transfused into the "celebrations" of the Church, wherein we encounter Christ himself. Inasmuch as he is always the living "Word of God," when we participate in a liturgical celebration where the Word of God is proclaimed, there

Jesus the "Word of God" speaks anew.

Hence, every liturgical celebration, and especially the Eucharist, becomes a new event, a continual renovation in space and time of the manifestation of the glory of the Lord Jesus, to transform every one of the faithful ever more — through the power of the Spirit — into his image. In a word, the liturgical celebration becomes "revelation celebrated."

The conviction of Christ's presence in his liturgical Word has become stronger in the faith of the Church in modern times, and especially after Vatican II. However, it can be traced as far back as the time of St. Augustine: "The Gospel is the mouth of Christ. He is seated in heaven, but he does not cease to speak on earth" (*Sermons*, 85, 1).

The pre-Vatican II German edition of the *Roman Pontifical* (1963) had this note: "Next is read the Gospel, in which Christ speaks to the people with his own mouth.... The Gospel should be actualized in the Church as if Christ himself were speaking to the people.... When Christ himself becomes present in person, that is, in the Gospel, let us set aside our walking stick because now we have no need of human support."

Jesus, the Lord of Glory, is present not only in a sacramental, real, and most concentrated way in the Bread and Wine of the Eucharist — which is the real presence par excellence in which Christ becomes our food — but also in the

Word that is proclaimed, and even before this in the very community that has come together. The presence of the Risen Lord in his followers is a key idea stemming from the words of Jesus: "I am with you always..." (Matthew 28:20).

This presence of Christ is not a local presence, a simple accident of space that involves no interrelation with us. It is a substantial presence of heart, mind, and will that enables us to be united with Christ personally.

The presence of Christ, who first gives himself to us as Word and later as Eucharistic food, is a saving and dynamic presence. First, we "communicate" with him as the living Word of God and then as Bread and Wine.

"The faithful should be keenly aware of the one presence of Christ in both the Word of God — 'it is he who speaks when the Holy Scriptures are read in the Church' — and especially under the Eucharistic elements" (*Prologue* to the *Order of Readings for Mass*, Second Typical Edition, no. 46).

The Assembly Is Formed by God's Word

In the Old Dispensation, it was always God who gathered his people in assembly. He gathered together his chosen people in the desert by calling them out of Egyptian bondage (Deuteronomy 4:10). The initiative came from God through his spokesperson (Exodus 19:4).

On reaching Sinai, the people gathered at the foot of the mountain (Exodus 19:17). There they listened to the Word of the Covenant, which set forth God's plan to make of them a "holy nation."

In order that the Word proclaimed might be not only understood but also truly constitutive and form them into a people, Moses commented on it. The assembly showed its faith by uttering its "Amen" and by uniting with the ritual act of sacrifice carried out by Moses in their name: "the blood of the Covenant" (Exodus 24:8).

In the New Dispensation, Jesus came to gather together those who had been dispersed (Matthew 23:37) and lead them into the Kingdom of God (Luke 14:23; Matthew 22:1-14). He proclaimed the New Covenant by his Word and his act of love at the Last Supper, but he was betrayed in his will to call people together: the assembly of the Twelve was dispersed (Matthew 26:31; Mark 14:27).

Yet Jesus prayed for unity during his Passion (John 17:11-23) with loud cries and tears (Hebrews 5:7) and he was heard. In his Resurrection there was a "re-convocation" and it was now addressed to all human beings.

After Pentecost, the model of every Christian assembly is to be found in the early Christian communities characterized by their perseverance and assiduousness in the teaching of the Apostles, in common gatherings, in the Breaking of the Bread, and in prayer (Acts 2:42).

It is the Word of God that convokes the assembly of believers, builds it up, makes it grow, and fashions out of it a new people of the Covenant (*Prologue, op. cit.,* no. 7).

The Word proclaimed, above all in liturgical celebrations, is regarded as a memorial. It does not address present conditions alone but looks back to past events and forward to what is yet to come.

Thus, God's Word shows us what we should hope for with such a longing that in this changing world our hearts will be set on the place of our true joy (*Ibid.*).

In its turn the assembly evangelized by this Word is invited to evangelize others. Its members are exhorted to be the "bearers of the same Word in the Church and in the world, at least by the witness of their way of life" (*Ibid.*).

Reasons for Christ's Fourfold Presence

Generally speaking, then, there are four liturgical presences of Christ. Each constitutes a different mode of his presence for a specific purpose in our regard.

(1) *Christ's Presence in His Ministers.* The purpose of this presence is to link us physically with the fruits of our Lord's salvation. This is the way we can encounter Christ today and realize his saving effect in our lives. It represents our

insertion into the Paschal Mystery that took place once and for all some two thousand years ago.

(2) *Christ's Presence in the Assembly*. Our Lord promised that wherever two or three of his followers gathered in his name he would be in their midst (Matthew 18:20). When we come together to celebrate the Eucharist, which is the Greatest Prayer, Jesus prays with us.

In the words of St. Augustine, "Jesus prays for us and prays in us. He prays for us as our priest and he prays in us as our Head." He is among us as our Friend and Intercessor with the Father.

(3) *Christ's Presence in the Proclamation of the Word of God*. As the very Word of God, Jesus is the Author of all revelation. Thus, when the Scriptures are proclaimed, Christ is not merely spoken about. It is actually he himself who speaks to us today.

Jesus is present when both the Old and the New Testaments are read, but most especially when the Gospel is proclaimed. He is as present to us in the liturgical proclamation as he was to the people who came to hear him along the roads of Palestine.

(4) *Christ's Presence Under the Eucharistic Signs of Bread and Wine*. This presence is known as the presence of Christ par excellence, his Real Presence. One of the reasons for this name is that it is the only presence that remains. The Bread and Wine remain the Body and Blood, Soul and Divinity of Christ as long as they last

after they are consecrated.

This presence is intended to be the means for our close union with our brothers and sisters who share that presence with us. It provides our entrance into the Sacred Banquet in which the living memory of Christ's Passion is recalled, our souls are filled with grace, and we receive a pledge of future glory.

In his fourfold presence in the Eucharistic Celebration, Jesus is present (1) as our Mediator with the Father; (2) our Representative and Companion who pleads our cause; (3) our Teacher who leads us to him who is all Truth; and (4) our God who unites us to himself and to one another.

The People's Response to God's Word

In order for us to encounter Christ in the Word today, we need to make that Word intelligible to us. We need to become familiar with its language beforehand. The more we read over the readings before Mass, the more understandable they will be for us at the Liturgy of the Word and the greater appreciation we will have of Christ's presence in each particular Word.

A genuine familiarity with the Word of God will enable us to take fuller advantage of one of the outstanding qualities of that Word — its endless meanings. No matter how often we hear it, we always come to it anew. We can never exhaust what God is telling us in it.

We are not speaking here of purely individualistic encounters. We do not receive a message that is solely our own. We encounter God and Christ in the Church.

We receive a message that is for us within the context of the Christian community, which is the Church. We are enabled to perceive God's presence, and to understand his message to us today, only through the medium of the Church.

Anyone who wants to understand the event and the message must do so in union with the Church. We must listen with the Church if we would hear God's true Word.

Most important, from a subjective point of view, God's Word calls for a response on our part. Without a response it would be meaningless for us to listen to that Word. The sole reason that it is pronounced is to elicit a response.

We are called to respond positively to that Word. We must embrace it with an open mind and heart. It may call us to make sacrifices that we do not enjoy. Yet we must follow through and respond in conscience to it.

This is part of the implicit commitment we make when we assent to become a member of the assembly that comes to celebrate this Word and this Sacrament.

All who celebrate the Eucharist with a positive response through their full, active, and conscious participation in it are changed in some way. They are renewed, taken out of some aspect of themselves and made better. They come closer to becoming the person that God wants them to be. They put on Christ — taking on in their own inimitable way his attitude, his eyes, his ears.

They will then begin to see their lives in the light of God's eternal plan. And they will begin to carry out the task that he has set for them, a task that is theirs alone and no one else's.

"When God shares his Word with us, he awaits our response, that is, our listening and our worship 'in Spirit and in truth' (John 4:23). The Holy Spirit makes our response effective, so that we carry out in our lives what we hear in the celebration of the Liturgy: 'Be doers of the Word and not hearers only' (James 1:22).

"The liturgical celebration and the faithful's participation receive outward expression in actions, gestures, and words. These derive their full meaning not merely from their origin in human experience but from their point of reference: the Word of God and the economy of salvation.

"Hence, the participation of the faithful in the Liturgy increases to the extent that while listening to the Word spoken in the Liturgy they strive more diligently to commit themselves to the Word of God made flesh in Christ. They endeavor to conform their lives to what they celebrate in the Liturgy and then in turn to incorporate in the celebration of the Liturgy everything that they do in their lives" (*Prologue, op. cit.*, no. 6).

Conclusion

In the *Prologue* to the new *Order of Readings,* the Church sets down the dispositions that the faithful should possess during the Liturgy of the Word. They must listen to the Word of God with that internal disposition (that is, veneration of faith and love) and external disposition that will aid them to progress ever more in the spiritual life and insert them more deeply into the Mystery celebrated.

The historical salvific events of the past — irrepeatable, lived, and concentrated in Christ — are proclaimed by the Church convoked to a celebration in liturgical assembly. For while she evokes the stages of salvation with Christ, in Christ, and through Christ, she simultaneously invokes the power of the Spirit and praises the Trinity.

Indeed, it is the Holy Spirit who brings the Word of God into the hearts of the faithful: "The working of the Holy Spirit is needed if the Word of God is to make what we hear outwardly have its effect inwardly. Because of the Holy Spirit's inspiration and support, the Word of God becomes the foundation of the liturgical celebration and the rule and support of all our life.

"The working of the Holy Spirit precedes, accompanies, and brings to completion the whole celebration of the Liturgy. But the Spirit also brings home to each person individually everything that in the proclamation of the Word of God is spoken for the good of the whole assembly of the faithful. In strengthening the unity of all, the Holy Spirit at the same time fosters a diversity of gifts and furthers their multiform operation" (*Ibid.*, no. 9).

Chapter 7

Praying
the Responsorial Psalm

$\mathcal{I}$n his final recorded appearance to the apostles before his Ascension, Jesus spoke of what was written about him in "the Law, the prophets, and the Psalms" (Luke 24:44). Hence, the Church has always indicated, especially through the Liturgy, that there is a history of Christ in the Psalms.

Each Sunday in the Responsorial Psalm at Mass, the liturgical assembly is invited to read a page of this history. In doing so, every one of us can discern some aspect of Jesus and hear his voice on a matter of importance to us.

However, in order for this result to be attained we must participate fully, consciously, and actively in the Responsorial Psalm, which occurs after the First Reading in the Liturgy of the Word.

Liturgists tell us that the Responsorial Psalm

together with the Alleluia Acclamation before the Gospel is the most important part of the people in the Proper of the Mass for it functions as a kind of commentary on the Scriptures just proclaimed. It draws the soul to arrive at the interpretation of the Reading intended by the Church.

Indeed, the Responsorial Psalm is the only psalm used at Mass for its own sake rather than to accompany an action. It is the Word of God used as a response to the Word of God. That is why the Church insists that it may never be replaced by a non-biblical text.

However, it is evident that in many cases, the people do not even know what is happening as the Responsorial Psalm goes flitting by during the celebration. This is even truer when the Responsorial Psalm is sung by the cantor with only a refrain relegated to the people.

What is needed is to make information available to all about the function of this part of Mass, so that they will be able to take advantage of the music and the words to enter into the theme of response. The following observations may be of help in this respect.

Canticle of the Covenant

Throughout the history of the Church, which is the people of God (in figure in the Old Testament and in fulfillment in the New), we find a pattern. God "speaks" to his people by accomplishing wondrous deeds for them. The people respond by celebrating these wondrous deeds.

God guides the people of the Exodus across the Red Sea. Miriam, following the lead of Moses her brother, celebrates the Lord who has cast horse and rider into the sea (Exodus 15:1, 21).

God delivers Hannah from her sterility by giving her a son, Samuel. Hannah responds by celebrating the Lord who enables a sterile woman to give birth (1 Samuel 2:5).

God delivers Tobit from blindness. Tobit responds by celebrating the Lord who lets his light rise over Jerusalem as well as in the hearts of his people (Tobit 13:11).

In New Testament times, God blesses Mary's virginity by letting her become the Mother of Jesus. Mary responds by glorifying the Lord and exulting in God her Savior, in Jesus whom she is bearing (Luke 1:46-55).

In accord with these examples, the Responsorial Psalm plays a similar role in the liturgical celebration. The Word proclaimed recalls God's wondrous deeds of old. The assembly celebrates these wondrous deeds and actualizes them in the celebration. It responds to the God of these wonders with the Responsorial Psalm.

The Word proclaimed is the word of the Covenant. The Responsorial Psalm is the canticle of the Covenant. It prepares for the Covenant, helps us enter into it, chants the grace of the Covenant, and asks God to keep us in it.

The Psalter: the Christian Prayer Book

In order to sing the Responsorial Psalm well, we should get to know something about the Book of Psalms or Psalter. It has become the book of Christian prayer, the compendium of the entire biblical message.

According to St. Thomas Aquinas, the Psalter — in contrast to the other biblical writings — "embraces in its universality the matter of all of theology. The reason why this biblical book is the one most used in the Church is that it contains in itself all Scripture. Its characteristic note is to restate, under the form of praise, all that the other biblical books express by way of narrative, exhortation, and discussion.

"The purpose of the Psalter is to make people pray, to elevate souls to God through contemplation of his infinite majesty, through meditation on the excellence of eternal happiness, and through communion in the holiness of God and the efficacious imitation of his perfection" (*Exposition on the Psalms of David*).

The Psalms have been called with good reason a school of Christian prayer. These sacred songs cover a wide range of human experiences; they bring out our strengths and weaknesses, faith and wonderment, joys and sorrows.

The Psalms also show forth the prophesied glory of Jesus: for it is only in Christ that their full significance is revealed. The noted Bible scholar Joseph Gelineau has written that Jesus "personally described himself as the Lord whom God seated at his right hand (Psalm 109 -Matthew 22:44); as the stone rejected by the builders which became the head of the corner (Psalm 117 - Matthew 21:42); as he who comes, blessed in the name of the Lord (Psalm 117 - Matthew 23:39); he personally applied to himself on the cross the appeal of the persecuted psalmist (Psalm 21 - Matthew 27:46) and his prayer of trust (Psalm 30 - Luke 23:46)."

Thus, the Psalms set forth Christ's lowly coming to earth, then his kingly and priestly power, and finally his beneficent labors and the shedding of his Blood for our redemption. So Christological are they that they have rightly been termed "the Gospel according to the Holy Spirit." It is the Holy Spirit who inserted in them indisputable references to the life of Christ.

Poetic Qualities of the Psalms

The Psalms are among the world's best poetry. We all know "The Lord Is My Shepherd," but there are a host of others among the 150 Psalms that are just as classical.

The poetry of the Psalms contains rhythm, which is the recurrence of accented or unaccented syllables at regular intervals. But its outstanding trait is parallelism, which consists in the equal distribution or balance of thought in the various lines of each verse.

Synonymous parallelism is the repetition of the same thought with equivalent expressions:

"He who is throned in heaven laughs;
the Lord derides them."

Antithetic parallelism expresses a thought by contrast with an opposite:

"For the Lord watches over the way of the just,
but the way of the wicked vanishes."

Synthetic parallelism occurs when a second line completes the thought of the first by giving a comparison:

"When I call out to the Lord,
he answers me from his holy mountain,
 when I lie down in sleep,
I wake again, for the Lord sustains me."

By paying attention to the poetic aspect of the Psalms, we will be able to recite or sing the Responsorial Psalm with more understanding and greater participation.

Praying the Responsorial Psalm

The Psalms are not readings or prose prayers, even though on occasion they may be recited as readings. In Hebrew they were called "Songs of praise" and in Greek *Psalmoi*, that is, "Songs to be sung to the lyre." All the Psalms have a musical quality that dictates the correct way of delivering them.

Even when a Psalm is recited and not sung, its delivery must still be governed by its musical character. A Psalm presents a text to the minds of those singing it and listening to it, but it aims at moving their hearts.

In order to pray the Psalms with understanding, we must meditate on them verse by verse, with our hearts ready to respond in the way the Holy Spirit desires. As the one who inspired the Psalmists, the Holy Spirit is always present to those who in faith and love are ready to receive his grace.

Indeed, the singing of the Responsorial Psalm expresses the reverence that is due to God's majesty. But it should also be the expression of a joyful spirit and a loving heart, in keeping with its character as sacred poetry and inspired song and above all in keeping with the freedom of the children of God.

The Responsorial Psalm is a different prayer from one composed by the Church. The inspired Psalmist often addresses the people as he recalls the history of God's people; sometimes he addresses creation; and at other times he even introduces a dialogue between God and the people.

In praying the Psalm we should open our hearts to the different attitudes that may be expressed, which vary with the type of writing to which it belongs (Psalms of Grief or Trust or Gratitude and the like). Although the Psalms originated many centuries ago in the East, they express accurately the pain and hope, the unhappiness and trust, of every people and every age and country, and celebrate especially faith in God, revelation, and redemption.

In the words of another renowned Scripture scholar, Andre Choracqui, "We were born with this book [of Psalms] in our very bones. A small book; 150 poems; 150 steps between death and life; 150 mirrors of our rebellions and our loyalties, of our agonies and our resurrections."

The Psalms have great power to raise minds to God, to inspire devotion, to evoke gratitude in favorable times, and to bring consolation and strength in sad times. They constitute an inexhaustible treasury of prayers for every occasion and mood in a format that is true to the whole tradition of the History of Salvation.

Thus, we should strive to pray the Responsorial Psalm with the best of intentions both at home and at Mass. It will then become for us an opportunity to rediscover our own humanity, in its anguish, its rebellion, its violence, and its reconciliation as well.

It will become for us an opportunity to rediscover more broadly the whole of history, for example, those men and women who also struggle, who suffer, who cry out, who hope, and who pray in the four corners of the earth.

Finally, it will become for us an opportunity to encounter Christ mysteriously present in the heart of this humankind in which we find ourselves.

Chapter 8

Appreciating
the Gospel Procession

$\mathcal{A}$t some celebrations of the Eucharist, the participants are treated to a colorful rite during the Liturgy of the Word. During the singing of the Alleluia or other chant before the Gospel, the deacon (or in his absence the priest) puts incense into the censer and says the prayer "Almighty God, cleanse my heart and my lips that I may worthily proclaim your holy Gospel."

He then takes the Book of Gospels from the altar and carries it in solemn procession to the lectern, preceded by the acolytes holding the censer and two lighted candles. At the lectern, the deacon opens the Book and proclaims the Gospel.

When we are fortunate to witness and be part of this rite, we are struck by its beauty and its significance. It is the perfect lead-in to one of the highlights of the Mass — the Gospel Proclamation.

Unfortunately, very few Catholics are aware of this wonderful ceremony and the meaning it holds for us. First, it is rarely used. Second, even when it is used, it is almost never explained.

For some reason, processions seem to be unpopular in some Church circles, although in our everyday lives there are all kinds of processions (or parades, as they are commonly called).

Every other week, it seems, we see or hear of a parade for some organization or other, filled with fanfare, dignitaries, marching bands, and happy people, bringing joy and legitimate pride to a segment of the populace. A parade has become a veritable American institution and a marvelous means for unifying people.

The Processions at Mass

Why then is the use of processions so seldom implemented in the Liturgy? Certainly, the Church herself does not restrain us from doing so. Indeed, in the wake of the liturgical reform, the Church still calls for five processions at each Mass — at the Entrance, at the Offertory or Preparation of the Gifts, at the Communion, and at the Dismissal, as well as at the Gospel. Each of these processions has its reason for being.

A brief consideration of the other processions and their effect on each member of the assembly may give us a better insight into the Gospel Procession.

The Entrance Procession enables us to enter in spirit with the other participants at the Eucharistic Celebration — those who minister at the altar: priest, deacon, ministers, readers, extraordinary ministers, and choristers. It also allows us to acclaim Jesus (in the person of the priest) who comes to reenact and re-present his saving sacrifice and to invite us to partake of his sacrificial meal — to become one with him and in him.

The Offertory Procession enables us, represented by a few of our members, to bring to the altar the gifts from which the sacrifice will be effected — the bread and wine as well as the monetary offerings of the assembly. At the same time, our representatives also symbolically carry with them our joys and sorrows, hopes and fears, work and leisure, and the whole of our everyday lives in the coming week. All will be turned into God's gift to us in this celebration — Jesus.

In the Communion Procession we ourselves physically take part in going to acclaim Jesus in the Eucharist, the Jesus who comes to us in a special way. We receive him from his minister, thus sharing in this sacred meal that brings all of us in this assembly together and concludes the sacrificial part of the rite. It also gives us a particular bond with all those who have received Christ in Communion over the centuries as well as in our own day.

At the Recessional Procession we join in singing while the other participants exit the sanctuary and the church. It is our farewell to them and to one another for their roles in reenacting and re-presenting the wondrous mystery of the Mass. It may be likened to the closing song of any gathering, the wish that all will get home safe, the final touch on a human ritual.

The Importance Accorded the Gospel

From the earliest times, the Gospel Proclamation in the Liturgy was accorded a special place of honor. The Book from which it was read was decorously illuminated with silver and gold lettering and ornately bound. Only a member of the clergy could proclaim the Gospel.

Then the etiquette of court ceremonial was applied to the Gospel Procession — acolytes with candles, incense, torches, and bowls of fire led the way. These effects added up to a completely human way of showing forth the triumph of Christ over sin and death.

At the same time, such natural trappings were the human signs to indicate that Christ himself comes to us in the Gospel. He comes to proclaim his Word to us here and now and to enable us to apply that Word to our lives today.

Jesus has accomplished a death-defying and life-fulfilling deed on our behalf in his passion, death and resurrection, and we naturally want to acclaim him for it. In the Book of Revelation (15:3-4), the victorious Lord is pictured as a Lamb who was accorded unrestrained acclaim:

"Mighty and wonderful are your works, Lord God Almighty! Just and true are your ways, O king of the nations! Who will not fear you, Lord, or glorify your name? For you alone are holy. All the nations will come and worship before you, for your righteous acts have been revealed."

This is the acclamation Christ is given in the Gospel Procession, and there is nothing extraordinary about it. On a modified scale and in countless ways in our society, we often acclaim the achievements of others. A great star delivers a flawless performance on a Broadway stage and is brought back for curtain call after curtain call with bravos and hurrahs. An outstanding athlete hits a dramatic home run and the fans are on their feet with a thunderous ovation that calls him out of the dugout to take a bow.

We do this naturally. Somehow such action identifies us with the person being extolled and with the deed that he or she has accomplished. We extol the person for his or her performance and we take both to our hearts and make them our own.

In similar fashion, we acclaim the office of a person. The President of the United States comes to address us. He follows a rigid protocol and is introduced to the stirring strains of "Hail to the Chief." Everything is done with a flourish. Or a Queen of England comes to town and is acclaimed with pomp and circumstance.

By cheering such officials, we become one with them and with what they represent. While lavishing them with praise, we give ourselves courage, hope, and life.

Something similar is communicated by the Gospel Procession. Obviously this is a good that is favored by everyone. We all eagerly seek such effects in our liturgical services. Why then is the Gospel Procession so seldom seen in our liturgies?

Possible Reasons for Disuse

Possibly the chief reason for the lack of use of this rite at Mass is an uneasiness on the part of Liturgy planners with anything that smacks of pomp in our worship. Somehow, a procession seems to look too artificial or too phony — something that is not really in accord with the life we know in America.

Yet, as we have just indicated, there are many similar occasions in our lives. The key point is that in those other occasions the acclamations and parades are more spontaneous; they flow out of an event in a very natural fashion.

Why, then, can we not make such acclaim flow naturally from the liturgical event in which we are taking part? If we can honor human beings for their deeds, we can certainly honor the God-Man Jesus Christ for his mighty acts — which dwarf all others!

Another reason for the disuse may be the fear that the procession will be ragged and unprofessional and not serve the end for which it was intended. It takes practice to perform the ceremony correctly, and the participants are often not accessible to the priest and deacon who will be involved in the ceremonial.

So it all comes down to lack of time and preparation — which in many cases can be reduced to lack of interest. Hence, we must interest all involved in this ceremony — especially the acolytes, music directors and assembly — if we are to make this ceremony the highlight of the Liturgy of the Word that it truly is. Demeanor, music chosen, and degree of participation are of the utmost importance in this regard.

We must get the point across very graphically that Christ is present among us — as truly as he is when the Blessed Sacrament is solemnly carried in procession around the Church on Holy Thursday or the Feast of the Body and Blood of Christ. Hence, what we do at the Gospel Procession we do to Christ himself. We could probably learn a lot in this regard from our brothers and sisters in Eastern Rite Catholic Churches.

Still another reason for the disuse may be a latent distaste for all show of triumphalism on the part of today's hierarchy. They fear to give the impression of a regal, wealthy, aristocratic faith by emphasizing the idea of victory when the people's lives are so often intimately connected with defeat — poverty, hard work, troubles, and illness. They worry that a "triumphal" Liturgy may take on an air of unreality.

This is a valid fear — but the way to overcome such a possibility is to proclaim the reality of what we do at the Gospel Procession, not to avoid it. Those who truly believe in Christ's victory and what it means for us today are not overwhelmed by the failures of life. They are empowered to surmount all of them.

The Gospel Procession is a way of helping to overcome the disappointments of life. It gives us a glimpse in sign of the great victory that is ours even now and will be completely ours in eternity.

Real Meaning and Purpose

One of the many benefits of the Gospel Procession is that it helps to impart the real meaning and purpose of the Gospel proclamation at Mass. The Gospel reading (like all the readings) is not just an exercise in imparting information about God and his dealings with human beings. Neither is it a simple instruction on the teachings of the faith.

The Gospel proclamation is an event, a happening. It is an intervention here and now on the part of God the Father — through Jesus Christ and in the Spirit — in the life of this community gathered to celebrate the Eucharist. It is the continuation of the History of Salvation today.

Not only has God intervened in the Old Testament through his patriarchs and prophets.

Not only has he intervened in the New Testament through his only-begotten Son. He now intervenes in the lives of people today — mainly through the liturgical rites of the Church, which render Christ present in his Mysteries through the Holy Spirit.

In this communication, the Gospel has a privileged place, as shown by the unique liturgical features that surround it. The Gospel is the only reading preceded by a procession, by an acclamation, by a blessing, and by a prayer.

The Gospel is reserved for a person in Holy Orders whereas the other readings can be proclaimed by lay people. It is honored by lighted candles and incense and preceded by a call for attention: "The Lord be with you."

Then we all make the Sign of the Cross on our forehead, lips, and heart — that is, we consecrate with the sign of our redemption our thoughts, words, and sentiments. At the end, the one who proclaims the Gospel kisses the Book as an act of loving homage addressed to Christ himself.

The people of the assembly respond to the introduction to the Gospel reading with the words: "Glory to you, Lord," and at the end they utter one more acclamation: "Praise to you, Lord Jesus Christ" — both are addressed to Christ who by this action has come among us!

While the Gospel Procession takes place, an acclamation is sung — in honor of the Christ who comes to "evangelize" his people. He has already spoken in the other readings ("He himself speaks when the Holy Scriptures are read in the Church," *Constitution on the Sacred Liturgy,* no. 7). Now he will speak to his people in a way that is much clearer, more personal, more decisive, and more enriching than in the previous texts proclaimed.

The Acclamation comprises a short biblical sentence, praising God in his function of Teacher (Master) and preacher. It may also recall a scriptural thought proper to the feast or the day.

By entering into the spirit of this Gospel Procession, the people in the assembly become conscious of Christ's personal presence among them as surely as he walked among the people in Palestine two thousand years ago. He comes in his Word to proclaim his message anew — only this time it is to us, to our specific assembly and community so that he may direct that message and that Word to our particular problems, states, and desires. The Gospel Procession puts us in the ideal mood to open our hearts to Christ and to his Word!

A Truly Religious Experience

The Gospel Procession, when carried out properly and with a genuine liturgical sense, can impart a truly religious experience to the assembly and can lead to a truly religious experience on their part.

All the external details point to an inner

reality, a reality that is so overwhelming that unless we constantly remind ourselves of its presence we will not grasp it. Our mind will simply refuse to accept it unless we continually keep it before our eyes. The Procession is a graphic reminder that Jesus is present in our midst at the Gospel.

Indeed, Jesus is as present in the Liturgy of the Word as he will be in the Liturgy of the Eucharist — only in a different mode. Here he comes among us in his ever-living Word, and in the Liturgy of the Eucharist he comes to us under the appearances of Bread and Wine.

In both cases, it is the Risen Christ who is present, the Christ who came to reveal his Father to us and to free us from the shackles of sin and death by his own life, death, and resurrection.

The Gospel Procession can make all of this come alive for the assembly. The acolytes in that procession take our place; they are our representatives in going to meet Christ. We are going to welcome him. Our Acclamations say so. We want to hear his message, to take it to heart and assimilate it, and then to apply it to our lives today. We want to draw strength from it.

The whole proclamation of the Gospel is given a solemn and more important tone by the Gospel Procession. Instead of an exercise in public reading or hearing, it becomes what it truly is — a proclamation of the Good News to us, a proclamation carried out by a deacon or priest but one that is really directed to each of us by Jesus himself.

A few words at the end of the Second Reading in the nature of a Commentator's remark can set the stage beautifully for such a grace-laden event in our lives: "After listening to the Word God gave us through the Prophets and Apostles, let us now rise and go to meet and acclaim Christ as he comes to proclaim his Good News to us today."

The Word of God is never a dead letter written in some old dusty books but a living communication between living persons — God and us. This communication, effected through the power of the Spirit, makes us a New People in whom the Covenant made in the past is fulfilled.

Through our Baptism and Confirmation in the Spirit, all of us have been delegated as faithful messengers of God's Word by the grace of hearing that we have received. Our task is to be bearers of this same Word in the Church and in the world, at least by the witness of our way of life.

A regular practice of a reverent Gospel Procession together with a judicious use of incisive but unobtrusive introductory remarks will go far toward helping the people in this respect. We will begin to see and embody the riches that are waiting for us in the Mass and we will make the Mass part of our daily lives — to the benefit of the Church and the world.

Chapter 9

Professing the Faith

*O*n Sundays and major feasts, the Liturgy of the Mass calls for the recitation or singing of the Profession of Faith (or Creed) after the Homily and before the Prayer of the Faithful brings the Liturgy of the Word to an end. The assembly rises to its feet and its members proclaim their beliefs.

Such a recitation may sound odd to our modern-day ears that are unaccustomed to this kind of proclamation in common. The closest thing to it would be the Pledge of Allegiance that we may remember from our school days.

However, no matter how ragged it may seem, how artificial its recitation may appear, or how disconnectedly it may be uttered, the Creed is a most important part of our Sunday Eucharist. If we pay attention to its purpose and its content, it will help us participate more fully in the Eucharist and influence our everyday life.

Summary of the History of Salvation

The Profession of Faith constitutes a response to the Gospel. In it, after hearing Christ speaking to us, we express our steadfast attachment to his message in summary form.

The Profession of Faith is, therefore, much more than a simple enumeration of some articles of faith. It is a summary of the whole of Salvation History preached and accomplished by Jesus. Hence, it is fittingly used by the assembly to give response, acceptance, and adherence to the Word of God just pronounced in the Readings and Homily.

At the same time, its recitation recalls our privilege as baptized persons who, in Jesus, have become children of God and heirs of his kingdom. It reminds us of our role as members of a royal and priestly people, enabled to participate in the Sacrifice of the Mass by uniting our offerings to that of Christ, our High Priest.

In addition, we have been consecrated as victims with Christ and associated with the mystery of his death and resurrection (see Romans 6:3-11). We have been consecrated to the service and to the glory of the Father, the Son, and the Holy Spirit.

Perhaps more importantly, our Profession of Faith is a response not only to doctrinal precepts but to the person of Christ himself present in his Word. At the same time, it links the Liturgy of the Word with the Liturgy of the Eucharist by recalling the Mysteries of Faith that will be reenacted and proclaimed in the Eucharistic Prayer.

The Creed is a development of the three questions concerning faith in the three divine Persons that were addressed to the candidates for Baptism and their threefold answer: "I believe."

(1) "Do you believe in God, the Father almighty?" — "I believe."

(2) "Do you believe in Jesus Christ, the Son of God, who was born of the Holy Spirit from the Virgin Mary; who died, was buried, and rose from the dead on the third day; who ascended into heaven, is seated at the right hand of the Father, and will come to judge the living and the dead?" — "I believe."

(3) "Do you believe in the Holy Spirit in the holy Church for the resurrection of the body?" — "I believe."

Because of its relationship to Baptism, the Western Church for a long time opposed the introduction of the Creed into the Mass. It was felt that, since the Creed is the Symbol of Faith — in other words, the sign by which believers are to recognize one another — that sign belongs most appropriately to the Sacrament of Initiation, which is Baptism.

It was also felt that the recitation of the Creed would be redundant, for the celebration of the Mass itself is already a profession of faith: "As often as you eat this bread and drink this cup, you proclaim the death of the Lord until he comes" (1 Corinthians 11: 26).

However, in time the proponents for the use of the Creed at Mass won out. Today, the Creed is an integral part of every Sunday celebration. The Profession of Faith that is used at most Masses is the Nicene Creed. In some Masses, the shorter Apostles' Creed may be substituted.

The Nicene Creed

The Nicene Creed is the profession of faith that the Council of Chalcedon (451) attributed to the Fathers of the Councils of Nicaea (325) and Constantinople (381). In reality, it may be the profession of faith of the Church of Jerusalem. This Creed has been used in the Mass since the 11th century.

This profession of faith insists on the divine and human nature of Jesus, who is consubstantial (that is, "one in Being") with the Father and Son of the Virgin Mary, true God and true man.

It also proclaims the Holy Spirit as "the Lord [and] giver of life." Finally, it presents the Church as "one" (with the unity of the three divine Persons), "holy" (with the holiness of Christ), "catholic" (open to all people), and "apostolic" (built on the faith of the Apostles).

Finally, in line with ancient Judeo-Christian traditions, the Creed declares that there is "one Baptism for the forgiveness of sins" (*A New Catholic Commentary on Holy Scripture*, no. 685e-i, p. 875).

The Apostles' Creed

The shorter Creed is called the Apostles' Creed because according to ancient tradition it goes back to the Apostles themselves. Its formulation is placed in Rome toward the end of the 2nd century.

The twelve statements of the Apostles' Creed are simple affirmations that can be substantiated in the Bible. Thus, this Creed may be termed a revelation through history. At its center lies the death and resurrection of Jesus, and it is bounded before and after by other historical events. Thus, the Creed delineates three historical stages:

First Stage: God-who-is-love, God the Father, source of life, gives his Son.

Second Stage: Jesus Christ is crucified, dies, and rises again.

Third Stage: The Father and the Son give the Spirit and establish the Church, which is the vehicle for fraternity, pardon, and life in the Spirit while awaiting the manifestation, the Day of the Lord, when he will come in glory at the end of time to judge the living and the dead.

This is the pristine faith as it comes through in the Gospels and Epistles of the New Testament. It is the "confession" to which we must hold fast (Hebrews 4:14) for it comes from the Apostles. The Creed transmits to us over a span of 2000 years "the faith that was once for all handed down to the holy ones" (and for which we must "contend" — Jude 3).

Trinitarian Theme

The Creed reiterates the Trinitarian theme that runs throughout the Eucharistic Celebration. The Liturgy always prays to the Father through the Son in the Holy Spirit.

The Eucharist begins with a profession of Trinitarian belief through the sign of the cross. At the end of the Introductory Rites, the Great Doxology (Gloria) sings lyric praise to the Trinity. In the Creed, the Church proclaims her explicit faith in the Trinity.

The Eucharistic Prayer, in its whole structure, manifests the Church's belief in the Trinity and then concludes with a Trinitarian Doxology.

At the end of the celebration, the people are blessed in the name of the Trinity.

The Profession of Faith — A Prayer of Praise

The Profession of Faith is an act of worship and is animated by a deep spirit of faith. Hence, it is altogether natural that the Liturgy should be the preferred, though non-exclusive, place in which Christians are called to proclaim their faith in Jesus Christ.

"In the Liturgy, slowly but constantly, the Profession of Faith (solicited by the living Word proclaimed in the liturgical action), which is spontaneous, personal, and dictated by the circumstances of the celebration, is oriented, in the light of the rule of faith, toward an objectivity and a synthesis in harmony with the common deposit of the faith" (A.M. Triacca).

The Creed is essentially an act of praise and hence it comes alive in an atmosphere of prayer. Even when it expresses a series of affirmations about God, it is essentially a prayer of thanksgiving. The basis for the confession of faith is the contemplation of the wondrous deeds of God and their salutary effect on the believer and the community.

Among other things, the Profession of Faith can serve as an excellent reminder to us that we are called to praise God more often in our prayer — whether liturgical or personal.

One of the forms of prayer that the Church has always made part of her repertory is the prayer of praise. It may also be called the prayer of adoration. As children of the "me generation," we may well have lost sight of this type of disinterested prayer. A quick look at it will show its beauty and power as well as its relevance to our lives.

The prayer of praise is universal. In using it, we are united with all who praise God including the song birds, splendiferous flowers and trees, bubbling brooks, and all the other enchanting elements in nature.

This prayer is also gratuitous. It is not concerned directly with the self in the manner of petitionary prayer. It has nothing to do with request but expresses only admiration and praise for God.

Indeed, we might say that this prayer is eternal. It will be the prayer with which we praise God forever.

Expression of Adoration

By the prayer of praise, we adore God (Father, Son, and Holy Spirit), that is, we recognize him as the Supreme Good, infinite in all his perfections: "The Lord, your God, shall you worship; him alone shall you adore" (Matthew 4:10).

We also acknowledge God as supreme Lord and Creator of all: "In the beginning... God created the heavens and the earth" (Genesis 1:1).

Third, we acclaim God as the Redeemer or Re-Creator of the whole of creation: "Behold, I make all things new" (Revelation 21:5).

Fourth, we exalt God as the Ultimate End: "I am the Alpha and the Omega, the first and the last, the beginning and the end" (Revelation 22:13).

Some of the perfections of God are: truth, infinite knowledge and wisdom, goodness, beauty, and love. Indeed, God is the Being beyond compare: "I am who am," he declared to Moses (Exodus 3:14). All other beings are but his creatures; they receive their being from God. He alone is eternal: "I live forever" (Deuteronomy 32:40). He alone is omnipotent: "Nothing will be impossible for God" (Luke 1:37); "O Lord, great are you and glorious, wonderful in power and unsurpassable" (Judith 16:13).

Hence, all human beings are called to praise God. We are to do so in various ways, among which are the following:

(1) with our whole life, by being what God intends us to be, faithfully carrying out his will, enabling his gifts to bear fruit in us, and making him known to others;

(2) with our prayer, both personal and liturgical. Indeed, we already give praise to God in many ways during the ordinary course of our lives. For example, we offer a prayer of praise:

(a) every time we recite the Glory Be to the Father;

(b) every time we say the *Te Deum* in the Liturgy of the Hours or at a ceremony marking the year's end;

(c) every time we utter the Canticle of Zechariah and the Canticle of Mary in Morning Prayer and Evening Prayer respectively;

(d) every time we pray the Responsorial Psalm at Mass when it is a psalm of praise.

Other Ways of Praising God

Sometimes we praise God directly. For example, Psalm 147:1 declares: "Praise the Lord, for he is good; sing praise to our God, for he is gracious; it is fitting to praise him."

Psalms 148, 149, and 150 all offer praise to God — for his goodness, his fidelity, and his justice, among other virtues.

At other times, we praise God in and through his creatures. After all, theologians tell us that God created the universe to manifest himself. The Book of Wisdom (13:1-5) rebukes pagans because they have failed to discover the Creator in and through his creatures: "For all were by nature foolish who were in ignorance of God and who, from the good things seen, did not succeed in knowing him who is.... For from the greatness and the beauty of created things, their original author, by analogy, is seen."

There are countless creatures, and each reminds us of God in its own way. But not all persons are touched by the same thing. Each of us must look for the things in creatures that remind us of the Creator — these may be the brightness of the stars, the freedom of the birds, the beauty of the flowers, the power of the waters, and the like.

We must keep the eyes of our heart open. If we do, we will discern hundreds of beautiful things that we have never thought of. We must cultivate an attitude of adoration on seeing the beauty and wisdom of God present in all his creatures.

We can also praise God in and through the

works of human beings. These works can indicate the greatness of God and serve as instruments that lead to him.

The Second Vatican Council teaches us that by our human work we are called to continue the work of creation, so that God may be glorified in his works:

"Human beings created in God's image received a mandate to subject to themselves the earth and all that it contains and to govern the world with justice and holiness; a mandate to relate themselves and the totality of things to him who was to be acknowledged as the Lord and Creator of all. Thus, by the subjection of all things to human beings, the name of God may be glorified in all the earth" (*Constitution on the Church in the Modern World*, no. 34).

By accomplishing our works we use the gifts God has given us: intelligence, will, and intuition, and we bring to fruition the energies found in nature.

We praise God with all we do that is good: (a) with the marvelous achievements of science — spaceships, computers, calculators, and the like; by these we manifest the wonder of God; (b) with the contributions of art — music, the figurative arts, and poetry among others; (c) by faithfully fulfilling the duties of our state in life whatever they may be; by these we show forth the infinite beauty of God.

Chapter 10

Participating in
the Eucharistic Prayer

℘rom the eleventh or twelfth century to the second half of the twentieth century, there was only one Eucharistic Prayer in the Liturgy of the Roman Rite, and it was known as the "Canon" of the Mass. In the early part of our century, the Liturgical Movement arose and led to a scientific study of the sources of the Liturgy as well as the psychology of religious worship.

Not surprisingly, the results indicated that the use of various formulas for the Eucharistic Prayer at Mass was decidedly better for all. Hence, since 1969 the Church has allowed other Eucharistic Prayers to be used in the Liturgy.

At present there are nine formulas for the Eucharistic Prayer that can legitimately be utilized by the priest in the United States (and in some countries there are a good deal more). Four are for general use and five are for special circumstances.

The variety of formulas does not have as its only purpose to avoid monotony. It also aims to impart a better grasp of the inexhaustible riches of the Eucharistic Mystery.

The whole Mass is an anamnesis, a commemoration, a memorial, a re-presentation of the passion and death, resurrection and ascension of Jesus — the Paschal Mystery.

This Mystery is invoked by the Entrance Song or Antiphon that suggests the theme of the feast, the Responsorial Psalm, and the Communion Song or Antiphon — though only from the particular viewpoint of the day. It is also mentioned by the Opening Prayer as a reason for confidence in our petition.

The Paschal Mystery is especially recalled in the Biblical Readings, which bring Christ present to us in his Word that recounts the History of Salvation. And it is again brought to mind in the Profession of Faith (Creed). By involving our faith, we become actors in this history that is ever unfolding.

Most of all, however, it is in the Eucharistic Prayer that the Paschal Mystery is recalled. Indeed, the Eucharistic Prayer is one long anamnesis. Hearing this prayer, we really relive the whole of Sacred History; our faith is fostered and we receive an incomparable degree of strength and comfort.

The People's Verbal Applause

At a quick glance, it seems as though the people have little to do with the part of the Mass when the Paschal Mystery is most emphatically re-presented. For the Eucharistic Prayer is uniquely the prayer of the president of the community, who voices the thanksgiving in the name of the people.

However, a closer look shows that there is a genuine dialogue within the Eucharistic Prayer. And far from being excluded from it, the people are very much involved in that dialogue.

All the texts of the Eucharistic Prayers have been drawn up by the Church to include the three principal movements of the liturgical dialogue:

(1) Preface and the people's Sanctus Acclamation ("Holy, Holy, Holy");
(2) Narrative of Institution including the Consecration and the people's Memorial Acclamation;
(3) Concluding Doxology (Minor Elevation) and the people's Great Amen.

It is important to note that at all three major points, the people have a telling role to play, helping them at the same time to offer with the celebrant. The assembly utters a vocal word of praise at these parts and gives verbal approval to what the celebrant has done and is doing.

This is similar to what happens in the case of speakers who give an address, deliver a lecture, or dedicate a memorial. They may be interrupted during their talk if the listeners are touched by their words and wish to show approval.

The first part of the Eucharistic Prayer proclaims the greatness, the glory, and the love of God, and the people respond with the "Holy, Holy, Holy."

Then the dialogue goes on at a deeper level. The Church recalls and makes present the saving deeds of God so that she may receive the thanksgiving (Eucharist) of Christ her head. For it is only in this way that she can give her gift of thanksgiving to the Father through the Son in the Holy Spirit. The people respond with the Memorial Acclamation, uniting themselves with the entire plan of God's love for the salvation of the world.

Finally, at the Minor Elevation the Church solemnly proclaims that glory, and the people respond with the Great Amen of assent.

The Sanctus Acclamation

At the beginning of the Eucharistic Prayer, we engage in an Introductory Dialogue with the celebrant. It provides the keynote of praise and thanksgiving that runs throughout this part of Mass.

The whole thrust of this dialogue is that we as a priestly people are with our Lord, whose presence is symbolized by the celebrant who through ordination has received Christ's "spirit."

Our attention is fixed on the heights where the risen Christ lives in glory, and we are intent on entering with him into his passage from the world to the Father. Hence, we give our assent to praise God.

We next come in after the Preface has succinctly outlined the reasons for this praise — the particular Mystery of the History of Salvation that is being celebrated on a given day or Season. We do this by the "Holy, Holy Holy," the Sanctus Acclamation.

This chant comes from Isaiah 6:3 — with an allusion to Daniel 7:10. It is our way of showing the unity of our Sacrifice of Praise with that of the Angels and Saints in heaven.

"In the earthly Liturgy, by way of foretaste, we share in that heavenly Liturgy which is celebrated in the holy city of Jerusalem toward which we journey as pilgrims...; we sing a hymn to the Lord's glory with all the warriors of the heavenly army; venerating the memory of all the Saints, we hope for some part and fellowship with them" (Vatican II: *Constitution on the Sacred Liturgy*, no. 8).

The second part of this Acclamation: "Blessed is he who comes in the name of the Lord," is preceded and followed by the words "Hosanna in the highest" (Psalm 118:25ff; Matthew 21:9). Better than any other Mass text, this Acclamation shows that the Eucharist is above all a Sacrifice of Praise.

With Christ, we offer God our praise. We forget ourselves and our finite existence and lose ourselves in the worship of the Divine Majesty. In so doing we simultaneously offer ourselves and every part of our lives to God.

The Sanctus Acclamation indicates that the earth as well as heaven is full of God's glory, and it will be filled with even greater glory as we continue our celebration of the Mass.

The Memorial Acclamation

After the Sanctus Acclamation we keep our minds on the wonders God has done for us in Christ by joining the celebrant in asking God to send his Spirit to make this sacrifice holy.

Then we find ourselves at the Consecration itself. We are transported in spirit to Calvary and reminded of Christ's sacrifice for us. His words and actions at the Last Supper are repeated in our presence, bringing us yet deeper into the Mystery of Salvation.

At this high point of the Eucharistic Liturgy, we are called to unite ourselves to the whole economy of salvation, the entire plan of God's love, for the salvation of the world: "Let us proclaim the Mystery of Faith," the mystery of our salvation.

It is not a matter of recalling one of the Mysteries of Faith but of recognizing that in the Eucharist the Mystery of Faith is realized, concretely recalled, and offered to us in our communion.

As a result, we fairly explode with praise and gratitude by using the words of one of the four Memorial Acclamations, expressing our belief that Christ came and suffered, rose in victory, and will return in glory to take us to him.

It is worth mentioning that instead of being addressed to the Father — as is the whole Eucharistic Prayer uttered by the priest — this acclamation is addressed to Jesus in keeping with the spontaneous movement of popular devotion.

The Memorial Acclamation has been introduced into the Liturgy only recently, but already it is a hit with most members of the assembly. It is also a wonderful manifestation at the very heart of the Eucharistic Prayer of the active participation of the faithful in the celebration of the Paschal Mystery, an expression of their baptismal priesthood.

Therefore, we should strive to proclaim it with inner understanding and outward reverence. For this Memorial Acclamation is a summary of what the Mass is. Christ has redeemed us, is with us now, and will come to us again in glory. It is our "little Easter" every day.

If properly appreciated, this Acclamation can sustain us amid the trials and tribulations of our everyday existence. It can become another golden opportunity given us by the Church for applying the Mass to our daily lives.

The Great Amen

At the conclusion of the Eucharistic Prayer the Church wants us to intervene once more with an external demonstration of our union with the Memorial that has taken place. For this purpose, she gives us the Great Amen to say or sing.

At this time, those of us who have participated fully are still imbued with the themes that make up the second part of the Eucharistic Prayer — a recollection of the saving events of Christ and the specification of those for whom the sacrifice is being offered: the servants of God, the relatives, friends, and benefactors of the members of the assembly who are Christians, as well as all people, living or dead. All have the opportunity, thanks to the Church and this sacrifice, to return to God and offer him the fruits of the redemption.

Yet this particular part flies by so quickly that few in the assembly can advert to what it means and even fewer know how to make the most of it.

The conclusion of the Eucharistic Prayer is a solemn proclamation of glory to the Father, through the Son, in the Holy Spirit — known as a doxology. It proclaims that glory in view of the whole plan of salvation that has been recalled and made present in this Eucharist and applied to this assembly here and now.

What is more natural than our ringing affirmation of this praise of God for his goodness and wondrous deeds! We say — through our Amen —that we heartily approve what has been done in this Eucharistic action in our name. We also show concretely that we have been part of the Thanksgiving and the Offering of Christ that have taken place.

We must realize that the Amen is a most important element in the Eucharistic Prayer. It says that both people and priest agree on the sentiments expressed in the Eucharistic Prayer.

A Personal Signature

At the end of the Eucharistic Prayer, we should be aware that our celebration has renewed the Covenant between the Father and the Church, of which our local assembly is a part. It has strengthened the bridal relationship between Christ and the Church. And it has provided the occasion for the Spirit to come again to the Church (as he once came at Pentecost) with a new infusion of supernatural life.

Hence, the Church can now — through her Head and Bridegroom and in the Holy Spirit — render all glory and honor to the Father. If we concentrate on the wonderful spiritual realities that God makes present to us in this sacrifice, we can enter into this Acclamation of glory joyfully and with our whole heart.

One of the prayers of the Eastern Rite Churches spells out some of the divine benefits better even than the Roman doxology: "Give [your servants] the power of the Holy Spirit, the confirmation and increase of faith, the hope of eternal life to come, through our Lord. Through him glory to you, Father, with the Holy Spirit forever."

The Great Amen is a time-honored way in which Christian assemblies have expressed their affirmation over the years. St. Justin the Martyr describes this same Acclamation in Roman Liturgies around the year 150.

St. Augustine has summarized this Acclamation in a nutshell. He tells us that saying "Amen" is like "putting our signature to the [Eucharistic] Prayer."

In the light of all this, it might be well for all of us to recall this graphic description of the Great Amen the next time we join in celebrating the Eucharist. It is sure to help us rise with enthusiasm at the Priest's doxology and sing or say our "Amen" with understanding, sincerity, and deep devotion.

It is, after all, the third and greatest of our Acclamations in the Eucharistic Prayer — our endorsement of the Liturgy we are taking part in. It enables each of us to make every Eucharist our very own.

Chapter 11

Partaking of the Lord's Banquet

*A*s already mentioned, the Communion Rite is the fifth minor division of Mass and enables us to achieve union with Christ. It also empowers us to attain union with our brothers and sisters in Christ.

In other words, the Communion Rite is the real conclusion of the Mass. It is the part when God gives a gift to us after we have presented our gift to him. In both cases, the gift is the same — Jesus Christ, Son of God and Savior of the world.

This part includes the Lord's Prayer, Sign of Peace, Breaking of the Bread, Lamb of God, Communion of Priest and People, Communion Antiphon or Song, Silence after Communion, and Prayer after Communion.

Culmination of Our Participation

The reception of Communion is, as it were, the culmination of our participation at Mass.

Eucharistic Prayer I indicates that those present "participate" by communicating in the Body and Blood of Christ.

As we have seen, to participate means more than one thing. It means above all to do all of one's part both externally and internally. But it also means to partake of what is on the table of the altar.

It is obvious that those present at Mass are called to make their participation complete and perfect by taking their proper portion of what is on the altar.

Communion brings us into closer union with Christ and with our brothers and sisters in him. It increases sanctifying grace, reduces our inclination to evil, and gives desire and strength to lead a good life. While remitting venial sin and guarding against mortal sin, Communion is a pledge of future resurrection and blessedness.

Preparing for Communion

The preparation of our soul for Communion is remote or proximate. Remote preparation entails a good Catholic life. Proximate preparation entails participation at Mass including the acts of prayer and devotion immediately before receiving Communion. These include the prayers of preparation in the Mass itself as well as more personal silent preparation as time permits and the Spirit moves you.

If we have the great misfortune to be in

mortal sin, we must first make a good sacramental Confession. We should also be sorry for our venial sins and strive to have them forgiven.

The preparation of our body for Communion has a penitential purpose and honors the sacred character of the Holy Eucharist. We must abstain from food and liquids (water excepted) one hour before receiving Holy Communion.

Since the fourth century it has been the custom to fast for some time before Communion. Through the Middle Ages, the rule was to refrain from eating or drinking from midnight on.

With the advent of the Second World War, circumstances often made it necessary to put off Mass until late afternoon or evening. As a result, Pius XII allowed various modifications of the midnight rule.

After the war, the continued proliferation of evening Masses made restoration of the rule impractical. Hence, in 1953 and again in 1957, Pius XII introduced further modifications, reducing the fast to three hours for solid foods and one hour for liquids.

However, those required to work on Sunday in our modern societies found it difficult to keep even this rule because it did not leave them sufficient time to eat supper and still be fasting for evening Mass. Hence, in 1964, Paul VI set the fast at one hour before Communion both for solid foods and for liquids (except water).

We should also dress in a way that shows reverence for the Sacrament. In this respect, common sense should prevail. What might be appropriate for the beach or the ballroom is not necessarily right for church.

At the same time, however, the "spirit" is more important than the "letter" on this point. It is more important to "come as you are" if the alternative is not to come at all!

Carrying Out the People's Parts

The surest way to participate in the Communion Rite is to carry out our parts during it in meticulous and devout fashion. By doing so, we will be ready to receive Communion in the way God wishes.

The Lord's Prayer. The Lord's Prayer is a petition both for daily food, which for us means also the Eucharistic Bread, and for forgiveness of sin, so that what is holy will be given to the holy!

We should join in this prayer with full knowledge that it is the prayer left us by the Lord and that it constitutes our formal request for Communion.

Sign of Peace. Before sharing the same Bread, we should be careful to express our Christian love for one another by the Sign of Peace. It is also our call for peace and unity in the Church and with all humankind.

Breaking of the Bread. The breaking of bread by Jesus at the Last Supper gave the entire Eucharistic Action its name in apostolic times. At Mass, the Bread is broken to be given to others. It signifies that we who are many are made one in the one Bread of Life — Christ.

Lamb of God. While the Bread is being broken, we sing or say the Lamb of God, a series of invocations in the style of a litany. This reminds us that Jesus is the Lamb of the New Covenant and we were saved by the precious Blood of Christ as of a spotless unblemished lamb (cf. 1 Peter 1:18-19). Every Mass is a memorial of the new Passover that brings forgiveness of sin and peace of mind and soul.

Communion of Priest and People. With the priest, we prepare to receive the Body and Blood of Christ by praying quietly. The actual rite of administering Communion is itself filled with meaning.

We are invited to receive Communion in words from Scripture: "This is the Lamb of God who takes away the sins of the world" (see John 1:29). "Happy are those who are called to his supper" (see Revelation 19:9).

We in turn use words of Scripture to accept the invitation: "Lord, I am not worthy to receive you, but only say the word and I shall be healed" (see Matthew 8:8).

Communion Procession. We have already touched upon the Communion Procession (Chapter 8). It accompanies the administration of Communion and expresses the unity, spiritual joy, and fraternal love of the people assembled to offer and communicate.

We must realize that at this point Holy

Communion far surpasses a private act of devotion. It is the action of the community whose members are praying for closer unity with Christ and with one another.

Communion Formula. The formula of administration and the response called for on our part are very clear and filled with meaning: "The Body of Christ." "Amen." "The Blood of Christ." "Amen."

St. Cyprian said: "Remember that it is not idly that you say 'Amen.' You are praying that you receive the Body of Christ.... You answer 'Amen,' that is, 'It is true!' Thus, keep in your heart what you profess with your lips."

Silence after Communion. There is room for private devotions here. After the procession, there is a time of silence and song, if desired. We can allot this time to private devotion — but in a communal setting. The Mass and Communion are never our private prayers. They are always communal.

Prayer after Communion. The Communion Rite comes to an end with the Prayer after Communion, which asks for the fruits of Communion for the whole Church. Our "Amen" evinces our desire to be united with others in our daily lives.

Paschal and Sacrificial Banquet

Vatican II, with evident reference to Communion, called the Mass "the Paschal Banquet in which Christ is received" (*Constitution on the Sacred Liturgy*, no. 47). Indeed, the Mass is wholly a Banquet, a supper, the richest prophetic signification of the Old Testament.

The ancient contents of that supper have been abolished and the Body and Blood of Christ have become its only contents. Yet the Mass is obviously a Banquet because it is essential that we feed ourselves in it.

Inasmuch as we partake of the Lamb in his true Passover, it is called the "Paschal Banquet."

Christ's Passover, his "passage" from this world to the Father, becomes the nourishment of human beings. Consequently, the Eucharist in all its expression is the perennial, continual, and permanent Pasch of the Church. Whoever communicates eats the Passover of Christ.

The *Instruction on the Eucharistic Mystery* also recalls the fact that the Mass, besides being a "Paschal Banquet," is also a "Sacrificial Banquet": "[It is] a true Banquet in which, by means of the Communion of the Body and Blood of the Lord, the People of God participates in the goods of the Paschal Sacrifice" (*Eucharisticum Mysterium,* no. 3).

The ancient lamb of the Hebrew Passover meals was immolated, sacrificed. Christ too, as the true Lamb of God, completes his Passover by immolating himself. Those who communicate are nourished on Christ in his sacrifice. They are fed by Christ the Victim.

The *Instruction on the Eucharistic Mystery*

also declares: "Participation in the Lord's Supper is always Communion with Christ, who offers himself for us in sacrifice to the Father" (no. 3).

It is in this belief that Eucharistic Prayer IV states: "Look upon this sacrifice which you have given to your Church; and by your Holy Spirit, gather all who share this one Bread and one Cup into the one Body of Christ, a living sacrifice of praise."

It is also in this belief that the assembly invokes Christ the Victim as the "Lamb of God"; and the priest underlines the same sacrificial aspect of Communion by presenting the Sacred Host with the words by which John the Baptist pointed out Christ: "This is the Lamb of God who takes away the sins of the world" (see John 1:29).

And it is in this belief that the Prayer after Communion frequently stresses the sacrificial character of the Communion received.

The Sacrificial Dispositions of Christ

The consequences that flow from belief in the Mass as the Paschal and Sacrificial Banquet are extremely important for the Christian life. We who feed on the Passover of Jesus must continually feel committed to be involved in this Passover.

Hence, we should make of our lives a continual "passage" from sin to grace, from a level of mediocrity to a level of spiritual heights, unto the fundamental passage to the promised kingdom.

In addition, regarding Communion as the act of Christ giving himself to us is quite effective in helping us accept the love of Christ. Thus, Communion will create in us the proper sacrificial sentiments and dispositions of Christ, that is, the readiness to give ourselves to God without conditions, overcoming every obstacle and temptation.

We who have been incorporated into Christ through Baptism and made sharers of his divine life are nourished by his Body and Blood. Immersed in the death of Christ, we celebrate and renew this Mystery, uniting ourselves with it ever more deeply and increasing in ourselves the capacity and the dimension of the life given us.

Communion is the Bread of eternal life, that is, the Bread that nourishes, sustains, and renews and develops that divine life given us in Baptism until it comes to full fruition in eternity.

The Food of the Resurrection

We know that the Mass is offered in expectation of the coming of the Lord. At the same time, it helps deepen our conviction of this return and our salvific reward. All nine Eucharistic Prayers ask that those who are present may have eternal life. For example:

"For ourselves, too, we ask some share in the fellowship of your apostles and martyrs" (I). "Make us worthy to share eternal life with Mary, the virgin Mother of God" (II).

"May he make us an everlasting gift to you and enable us to share in the inheritance of your saints, with Mary, the virgin Mother of God" (III). "Father, in your mercy grant also to us, your children, to enter into our heavenly inheritance in the company of the Virgin Mary, the Mother of God, and your apostles and saints" (IV).

Indeed, even at the moment of Communion the Liturgy is preoccupied with calling to our minds the reality of this vision: "Happy are those who are called to [the Lord's] supper," says the priest as he holds up the Host before us.

By communicating in the glorified Body of Christ, we already participate in a certain way in the life of the Kingdom of God. The Eucharist that unites us in the glorified Christ becomes for us the "seed of immortality," "pledge and guarantee of the resurrection."

Jesus assured us of this: "[Those who eat] my flesh and drink my blood [have] eternal life and I will raise [them] up on the last day" (John 6:54).

We thus have the capability to surpass the barrenness of death: "Whoever eats this bread [my Flesh] will live forever" (John 6:58). In Communion we nourish ourselves with a Body and a Blood that have conquered death and bear within them the power of that victory.

In other words, the Eucharist is the food of the resurrection. And this has been prepared for and maturing ever since the day of our Baptism and our Confirmation. Immersed through Baptism in the Mystery of Christ's passion and resurrection, we have received the seeds of our own final resurrection.

At the moment of our Baptism, as St. Paul says, our heavenly body has been generated, the body of the Christian, which every Communion nourishes and causes to grow to maturity.

The Spirit given us at Confirmation, whose presence is recalled at every Mass, will cause these seeds to grow. He is the divine principle of the final resurrection, as he was for Christ. "If the Spirit of God who raised Christ from the dead dwells within you, then the One who raised Christ from the dead will give life to your dead bodies through his Spirit which dwells within you" (Romans 8:11).

Thanksgiving after Communion

Sometimes people say that the Church no longer wants us to give thanks after Communion. This is not even remotely the case.

The Church is all in favor of thanksgiving after Communion — but she wishes it to be part of the celebration. In other words, she wants the thanksgiving to be part of the service, to be communal in character — in accord with the whole thrust of the Liturgy and the reason for its celebration.

Insofar as we are part of the Eucharistic community at the time after Communion, our thanksgiving should be carried out in unison with

117

the whole community. This means by singing the Communion Song(s) or by reciting the Communion Antiphon or by entering into the spirit of the communal Silence or Praise after Communion.

This communal silent thanksgiving is then concluded with the communal prayer vocalized by the priest in the Prayer after Communion. Although the text varies from day to day, the meaning remains standard — requesting that Communion may commit us to a path that leads to eternal life.

Thus, we can best express by our lives the gratitude that we have toward God for his goodness in giving us this spiritual food and drink after we had offered Christ and ourselves with him in the Eucharistic Celebration.

This is the type of thanksgiving after Communion that the Church desires of us, as indicated in the *Instruction on the Eucharistic Mystery:*

"Union with Christ, to which the Sacrament [of the Eucharist] is directed is not to be limited to the duration of the celebration of the Eucharist. It is to be prolonged into the entire Christian life, in such a way that the Christian faithful, contemplating unceasingly the gift they have received, may make their life a continual thanksgiving under the guidance of the Holy Spirit and may produce fruits of greater charity" (no. 38).

Chapter 12

Living
the Liturgical Year

$\mathscr{A}$nother way of actively participating at Mass is to know and live the Liturgical Year. For the Mass and the Liturgical Year go hand in hand. If we celebrate one, we cannot but celebrate and participate in the other.

We are used to many kinds of divisions of the year — the civil year (January 1 to December 31), the scholastic year (September to June), the agricultural year (seed time to harvest), the commercial year (January to June and June to January), and the like. It should not be very surprising, then, that there is also a Liturgical Year.

It is a year that was fashioned by the Church over the centuries and under the influence of the Holy Spirit given her by Christ to enable her to proclaim the Good News throughout the ages to all peoples. Broadly speaking, this year is an orderly succession of sacred times and feasts established by the Church.

The History of Salvation

Indeed, the Liturgical Year has often been called "the masterpiece of the Holy Spirit." In the light of the Scriptures (inspired by the Holy Spirit), it sets forth the History of Salvation for us — and does so in such a way that we also become part of that history.

The first phase of this History shows us the Father's careful and continuous cultivation of his chosen people — all completely geared toward the coming of his Son into the world. In this phase, the gift of the Spirit is a personal one. It is given to certain prominent persons (high priests, kings, and prophets) for the benefit of the community over which they preside.

The second phase brings before us the Incarnate Word, Jesus Christ. He took flesh to effect our salvation. He proclaimed his divine message, accomplished our redemption by his cross and resurrection, and has been made a "life-giving spirit" who is a source of all grace and the primary cause of all spiritual life. For the humanity of Christ spiritualized and glorified in heaven gained the graces of the Holy Spirit (whose fullness Jesus possesses) that flow into our souls.

The third phase is the life of the Church since the first century in which the Holy Spirit plays a leading role. It is the function of the

Church, guided and vivified by the Holy Spirit, to bring us into contact with the Risen Lord and to ensure for us these graces, which will enable us to die to sin and to live as true members of Christ.

In this regard, the Liturgy plays a key role. In the celebration of the History of Salvation through feasts, the Church inserts us into that history and enables the Spirit to transform us into "other Christs."

Thus, the primary function of the Liturgical Year is to prolong the worship of and true dialogue with the heavenly Father that Jesus achieved by his life, especially his passion and resurrection. It enables us to encounter this saving Paschal Mystery of Jesus in signs and to render fitting worship to the Father in Christ and through the Spirit. At the same time, it empowers us to attain the saving benefits of his sacrifice that Jesus obtained once and for all on the cross.

Every Sunday the Church keeps the memory of our Lord's Paschal Mystery. She continues to sanctify time and to consecrate it to God by the Liturgical Year. Within the cycle of a year she unfolds the whole Mystery of Christ, from the Incarnation and Birth to the Ascension, the day of Pentecost and the expectation and coming of the Lord.

Through the Liturgy, these events of Christ's life are really present to us today. They are our way of encountering Christ — not in the flesh as people once did along the roads of Palestine but in his Mysteries. And this encounter has the power to sanctify us just as it did those whom he met during his time on earth.

Outline of the Liturgical Year

The Liturgical Year comprises the Seasons of Advent, Christmas, Lent, Easter, and Ordinary Time. During these sacred Seasons the Church forms us in the faith by means of pious practices, instruction, prayer, and works of penance and mercy.

Nov./Dec.	Advent Season (4 Sundays before Christmas) We Prepare for the coming of Jesus, who is here and yet to come.
Dec. 25	Christmas (Birth of Jesus)
Dec./Jan.	Christmas Season We celebrate the gift of our Father's love: Jesus is our brother and our Lord. Feast of the Holy Family (Sunday after Christmas) Feast of the Epiphany (2nd Sunday after Christmas) (Jesus shows himself to the world)
Jan./Feb.	Ordinary Time (between 5 and 9 weeks) With Jesus we enter into the work of his Body, the Church.
Feb./Mar.	Lenten Season We do penance and root out our faults

	so we may rise with Christ as new persons at Easter.
	Ash Wednesday (40 days before Easter)
	5 Sundays
	Palm Sunday (Christ's Solemn Entry into Jerusalem)
Mar./Apr.	Holy Week culminating in Christ's Resurrection on Easter
	Easter Season (5 Sundays)
	Sharing in the new life of Christ, we are filled with his Spirit.
Thursday in May	Ascension Thursday (40 days after Easter)
	7th Sunday of Easter
May/June	Pentecost (50 days after Easter, sending of the Spirit)
May/June	Ordinary Time (continuation of the preceding season between Epiphany and Lent, this season counts 33 or 34 Sundays in all)
	Guided by the Spirit of Jesus, we build the kingdom of God by our lives.
	Feast of Christ the King (Last Sunday of the Liturgical Year)

Season of Advent

During the Season of Advent, the Liturgy invites us to participate in the hope of Israel and its thousand-year expectation — in order to prepare us to hear the tidings of great joy announced by the angels at Christmas.

We are encouraged by the Church to recall the three greatest figures who originally prepared for Christ's coming in the Flesh. By concentrating on them, we can benefit from his coming to us in Mystery at Christmas and in Majesty at the end of the world: the Prophet Isaiah, John the Baptist, and Mary the Mother of God.

Each of these three can show us the virtues we should have in preparing for Christmas and bringing Christ into our lives and to the world.

Among these virtues are the following: listening to God's Word without preconception, understanding it without pretense, and responding to it without reserve.

The most important virtue for Advent is to put God first in our lives, to carry out his will, and to lead others to him.

We know that all the promises God made have been fulfilled in Jesus. "However many are the promises of God, their 'Yes' is fulfilled in him," declared St. Paul (2 Corinthians 1:20). We do not await the Messiah that Israel awaited; our hope is new.

Aware that salvation has been accomplished, we await the day when it will be revealed by the new coming of the Lord. This will take place on the day when he will be glorified in all those who have believed in him and he will establish the Kingdom of his Father: "Come, you who are blessed by my Father. Inherit the kingdom prepared for you from the foundation of the world" (Matthew 25:34).

We await this Kingdom and we prepare for it by our witness. For before the Lord's final coming the Good News of salvation must be preached to all nations.

By preparing for the Lord's coming time and again at Christmas, we prepare for his final coming, which will be decisive for each of us and for all human beings: "Now we watch for the day hoping that the salvation promised us will be ours when Christ our Lord will come again in his glory" (Preface I of Advent).

Season of Christmas

The feasts of the Liturgical Year bring before our minds the sign of some hidden sacred reality that must be applied to all of us. During the Christmas Season this hidden sacred reality is the light, the life, and the joy beaming from Christ, the "Sun of Justice," upon humankind lost in the darkness of ignorance and sin (Malachi 4:2).

We must honor this Mystery not as something that happened some two thousand years ago but as something present today. For while the act itself (Christ's birth and manifestation) is past, its effects are very present.

Christ is present in the Mystery of Christmas, constantly interceding for us and communicating himself in holy symbols. Thus, we are to meditate on and celebrate the Christmas Mystery as happening to us now and embrace its mystical effects with an open heart.

In the glorious feast of Christmas, we commemorate the coming of Christ in the flesh (in history) to save the world. We celebrate now in the Liturgy (in mystery) to apply that salvation to each individual. Finally, we look forward to the coming of Christ on the Last Day (in glory) to complete this salvation in each of us.

In Christ we encounter the Father who is gracious to us, comforts and consoles us, and accepts us as his adopted children. By entering fully into the Christmas spirit, we can strengthen our faith, hope, and love.

Season of Lent

The word Lent is an ancient word for Spring. The Season of Lent is a time for new life to appear in us and for old negative attitudes to disappear. It is the period for us to prepare to celebrate the Paschal Mystery of Christ.

During Lent we should keep in mind three dominant themes: Cross, Repentance, and Baptism.

The Cross recalls the supreme law of Christian life: death in order to live. It also brings with it a positive aspect of conquest and salvation. Through his Cross, Christ gave impetus to all the positive works of humankind. It is the Cross that enables us to build the world as God's co-workers, while eschewing all forms of evil.

Repentance is ultimately total change of self, an intimate renewal of one's person, a reappraisal of one's understanding, one's judging, and one's living. It is a turning from self to God.

The practices by which this is done are usually numbered as prayer. mortification, and almsgiving. However, they are really as many as there are people. Anything that truly brings about this conversion is valid.

Today, we might mention such things as working for social or individual justice, performing spiritual and corporal works of mercy, and a renewed interest in the Mysteries by which we are reborn as children of God.

During Lent, we are called to remember our Baptism — to deepen the sense of our condition as baptized people. We do this primarily by clinging to Christ, by choosing to follow him more closely, by becoming in some sense "other Christs."

We are guided in this by our Baptismal grace that illumines us by faith, renews us by conversion of life, rules out all compromise with evil, leads us to community of life and responsibility with our brothers and sisters in the world, and orients us for the Lord's return in glory.

We must be open to instruction in the Faith — through hearing, reading, study, good conversation, and any type of positive communication (film, art, music, etc.).

We must be people who listen — to others, to our consciences, to the world, and most of all to the living Word of God in the Bible.

We must be doers. After truly listening, we must respond and put into practice what we have learned. In this way we will bring about that inner conversion to God which is the most fitting preparation for Easter.

Season of Easter

During the Season of Easter, we rejoice in Christ's saving sacrifice and his glorification through his resurrection in which we share. By his passion and resurrection, Jesus has transformed the world. He has overcome evil, sin, and death in such an absolute fashion that all who come into the world are ensured of life — eternal life through faith in him.

The vehicles through which this transformation takes place are the Mass and the Sacraments (and Sacramentals). The Sunday Mass consecrates the particular joys and sorrows of our community as well as those of the whole world.

By replenishing ourselves at this source weekly, we keep in touch with Christ and live a completely Christian spirituality in the world. The main point is to make sure that we advance the progress of the world toward Christ during the rest of the week.

However, even when we direct our prayers and actions to bringing about the coming of God's Kingdom, the sad fact is that few of us are genuinely moved in the depths of our hearts by the wild hope that our earth will be recast or transformed. Easter means that we must revive this hope in our hearts.

We must realize that each of us contributes our share to the building up of the Body of Christ by our incorporation into the Church and by our works. And by building the world in a positive way, we are building up the Body of Christ.

Every process of material growth is ultimately directed toward his Second Coming, and every process of spiritual growth is directed toward Christ. Christ is waiting to receive the fruit of our work — and that fruit is not only the intention behind my action but also the tangible result of my efforts.

Season of Ordinary Time

Ordinary Time is the name given to that part of the Liturgical Year that does not fall within one of the major seasons — Advent, Christmas, Lent, or Easter. It numbers thirty-three or thirty-four Sundays (depending on the date of Easter) and is assigned to two periods of the year — Epiphany to Lent and Pentecost to Advent.

At this time the Church continues to celebrate our Lord's resurrection — but in its application to our earthly lives. The Time after Epiphany covers the beginning of Christ's preaching, his Baptism, and his first manifestation. The

Time after Pentecost covers Christ's Public Ministry of healing and preaching.

Ordinary Time unfolds Sunday by Sunday without any particular celebration, except for a few feasts of devotion or of Saints. It is characterized by two themes: that of the Sunday and that of the Church.

Thus, Ordinary Time is a period of growth for all who follow the Liturgy. It is a time for accentuating all the Christian virtues. But it has nothing of the extraordinary about it.

It is rather easy for us to get excited about the major Seasons of the Liturgical Year — there is much to think about and more to do. But what is there to get excited about in Ordinary Time?

Herein lies one of the major difficulties about the Christian life in our day. We are called to live fully the "today" — without complaint and without looking for instant "pick-me-ups."

We must dare to live every day in all its monotony and ordinariness. For it is by our fidelity to ordinary things that the majority of us are to be saved.

This is the paradox presented by the sanctity that, poor and unobtrusive, daily bears out the truth of the Beatitudes. As the saying goes: "Sanctity is made up of little things — yet sanctity is not itself a little thing!"

Fortunately, we do not have to do this alone. We are aided in this silent and gradual spiritual growth by the Holy Spirit. It is the Spirit who helps us live each Sunday, and each day, to the full. It is the Spirit who makes of our seemingly ordinary lives an eternal offering to the glory of God!

Threefold Fruit

We see, then, that it is up to us to take hold of the Liturgical Year and live it to the full, so that we may derive from it its threefold fruit — to know Jesus, to imitate Jesus, and to live in, with, and through Jesus.

(1) *To know Jesus.* The Liturgical Year enables us to attain an ever greater knowledge of Jesus until we reach the "unity of faith and knowledge of the Son of God, to mature adulthood, to the extent of the full stature of Christ" (Ephesians 4:13).

In knowing Jesus we will come to know the Father: "Philip, whoever has seen me has seen the Father" (John 14:9). And in this knowledge of Father and Son is eternal life: "This is eternal life, that they should know you, the only true God, and the one whom you sent, Jesus Christ" (John 17:3).

(2) *To imitate Jesus.* Imitation is the sincerest form of flattery. All Christians are called to be other Christs, adopted children of the Father. Growing in the knowledge of Jesus through the Liturgical Year will enable us to put on his mentality (to learn to imitate him): "Have the

same outlook among you that Christ Jesus had" (Philippians 2:5).

Naturally, such an ideal is never fully attained on earth. This is why each year the Church calls us to begin anew to encounter Jesus in his Mysteries and imitate him in our lives.

(3) *To live in, with, and through Jesus.* Living in accord with the Liturgical Year will enable us to live in Christ (John 15:4). Specifically, this means doing what he commands. It means "putting on Jesus Christ," in St. Paul's phrase, so that it is Christ who lives in us (Galatians 2:20).

Helpful Attitudes

We are aided in obtaining this threefold fruit by the following attitudes. We must make the Mass a part of our life situation. We must bring to it our experiences, conditions, joys, sorrows, and hopes and combine them with the wealth of spirituality found therein.

The Mass will take our experiences and transform them into means of growing in Christ. It will help us to build a world for Christ, a world ready for his Second Coming.

We must also strive to have a biblical mentality. This means we must accept the fact that God speaks to us in words and actions. Every event, every encounter, every conversation, can be carrying a message from God to us — if only